Sew a Small Doll and Her Clothing

Sherralyn St. Clair

COPYRIGHT

Copyright 2012 Sherralyn St. Clair

You may sell or give away as many of the dolls or the doll clothing as you can make by yourself. The dolls or clothing cannot be mass produced without my permission. You may make as many copies of the patterns as you need for your own use. You may not give away or sell the patterns or the instructions, or kits containing the patterns or instructions.

V 13-09-09

ISBN-13: 978-1470074357

ISBN-10: 1470074354

ACKNOWLEDGMENTS

Back cover: Scooter from Dollspart Supply; Tea set from Ellen's Hand Painted Treasures

INTRODUCTION

I have always loved small dolls. I think that their size is charming. They are easier to display and store than larger dolls. I seldom need to buy fabric for them, because their clothes can be made from fabric scraps. Their accessories are easy to find. I have been collecting small doll props for years. If you look at the doll pictures below or on the back cover, you can see the dolls using some of the many accessories that I have in my collection.

Small dolls are wonderful companions for children. They are just the right size for carrying along on outings and make great travel dolls. I think that they are a good choice for creative play. These little dolls also make wonderful dolls for larger dolls such as the many popular 18" (45 cm) dolls. The adventures of a doll's doll adds an interesting frame to imaginative games.

Because of my love for small dolls, I have been designing small cloth dolls for several years. On my website I offer patterns that contain three sizes of dolls. The pattern for the dolls themselves is sold separately from the garment patterns. Each garment pattern is also sold separately and contains three sizes. I have written this book for the dollmaker who would like to sew only one size doll and her outfits. I chose Florabunda from my three dolls for this book, because she is the middle size of my small dolls. Florabunda is about 7½" (19 cm) tall. The majority of small commercial dolls that I have found are about Florabunda's size. At the beginning of each outfit's instruction you will see a list of commercial dolls that can wear the pattern. There may be other dolls that can wear these clothes. I have tried the garments on the dolls that are listed.

At the beginning of each project I list the supplies and equipment that you will need to make the doll or garment. I also list the skills that that are explained in the instructions. Sometimes you are referred to the appendix called **Tools, Tips, and Techniques**. I discuss equipment and sewing techniques in this appendix. If you would like a free copy of **Tools, Tips, and Techniques** with color illustrations you can download it from the pattern page of my website, www.sherralynsdolls.com.

After each set of instructions are full size patterns for Florabunda or her clothing. The pattern pieces are labeled with the name of the doll part or clothing item. Copy or trace the patterns and use them in constructing your projects.

If you are using a copier, you want the patterns printed full size. Before cutting out your pattern pieces, check them against the patterns in the book to verify that they are the correct size.

I invite you to visit www.sherralynsdolls.com for sewing tips, ideas for doll accessories, free patterns for Florabunda, and free stories starring Florabunda. If you want to see a commercial doll wearing clothing from this book, check the small doll section of the Pattern Page or *Sew a Small Doll and her Clothing* on the Book Page. For free beginner friendly sewing patterns and fun craft projects check Florabunda's Page.

Email me at sherralyn@sherralynsdolls.com if you haves questions, suggestions, or just want to chat about dollmaking.

CONTENTS

Florabunda Doll 5

This pattern includes the doll itself as well as panties, a camisole, and sandals. If you have some previous sewing experience and enjoy sewing small things, this doll will be fun to sew. The pattern includes optional details like tiny fingers and toes. As an option there are instructions explaining how to prepare and print a fabric sheet with faces.

Gown, Smock, and Two Tiered Skirt..21

Use light cotton fabric or flannel to make a cuddly night time doll or use the smock and skirt patterns to make a stylish outfit. Instructions for a stocking night cap are included.

A-Line Dress, Jacket, and Bloomers..29

You can use your imagination to embellish this dress in many ways. The jacket and bloomers can be mixed and matched with other patterns. Instructions explain how to use either hook-and-loop tape or a zipper closure.

Pants, Skirt, and T-Shirt..39

You can outfit your doll with a typical kid's wardrobe. Patterns for adding optional pockets to the pants and skirt are included.

Princess Ballgown and Classic Dress...47

Use silky fabric and metallic lace for a royal ballgown or use cotton fabric and lace for a classic dress. There are instructions explaining how to make a crown to top-off the ballgown.

Shoes and Socks..55

You can purchase small doll shoes, but if you don't mind taking the time to make these tiny shoes they will add variety and charm to the doll's wardrobe. There are instructions for making a shoe last to help with construction.

Tips, Tools, and Techniques...61

This appendix provides additional details for some of the sewing techniques and procedures used in the patterns.

Sewing a Small Doll and Her Clothing
www.sherralynsdolls.com

Florabunda Doll

- Prismacolor® peach pencil and thin line air soluble pen for marking
- Boxes of waterproof colored pencils in primary colors and earth tones
- Thin line permanent markers in red, black, brown, and blue or brown for the eyes.
- White acrylic paint and a thin brush
- Optional powdered blush
- Polyester stuffing
- Pairs of ½" (12 mm) flat buttons and ⅝" (15 mm) flat buttons with two eyes for stringing arms and legs
- Unwaxed dental floss
- Seam sealant and wax paper
- Fabric glue stick
- 5 skeins of embroidery floss for hair in the color of your choice
- Permanent fabric glue
- Tear-away stabilizer
- Small piece of nylon tricot or T-shirt knit (panties and camisole)
- ⅛" (3 mm) wide elastic (panties)
- ¼" (6 mm) wide lace edging (panties and camisole)
- ⅛" (3 mm) ribbon (camisole and sandal)
- Optional small appliques (for camisole)
- Hook and loop tape (camisole)
- ¼" (6 mm) wide ribbon (sandal)
- Stiff felt (sandal)
- Tacky glue (sandal)

Equipment
- Basic sewing tools (see **Tools, Tips, and Techniques**)
- An open embroidery foot to use when following sewing lines for arms and legs
- One 2¼" (5 cm) or longer needle for stringing the arms and legs
- Stuffing tools such as a hemostat, chopstick, and an inexpensive paintbrush (use the smooth end)
- A cylindrical object (such as a medium point Sharpy Pen with the cap on) to keep the neck open while attaching the head
- Doll hairbrush, toothbrush, or fine comb to separate embroidery floss
- Bodkin for threading elastic through the casing (panties)
- Miniature clothes pins (sandals)

Supplies
- 100% cotton fabric in skin color of your choice
- Thread for sewing doll in slightly lighter color than fabric
- Optional darker thread for sewing the toes
- Optional freezer paper, Sulky® Sticky+, or quilt basting spray for printing the face onto fabric
- Optional masking tape to help with printing on fabric

Skills
- Color face with pen and pencil
- Attach head to body with ladder stitch
- Hand sewing fingers and toes
- Stringing arms and legs
- Prepare fabric and print face outline with a computer printer (optional)

Introduction

These instructions describe the construction of a 7½" (19 cm) Florabunda cloth doll and her panties, camisole, and sandals.

Symbols

The pattern pieces for Florabunda and her clothing are marked by a flower (✿).
Tips p (page number) refers you to the page in the appendix, **Tools, Tips, and Techniques**, that contains additional information about the sewing project.

Head

You may either trace the face of the doll onto fabric by hand or, you may copy the Face Page included with the patterns directly onto a piece of cotton fabric using an ink jet copier/printer.

Tracing the Face

Suggestions for tracing the face are found in the **Tools, Tips, and Techniques** section of the book under "Marking Fabric." **(Tips** p 66) When you have traced the face, go to the section titled "Coloring the Face" to complete the doll's face.

Printing the face on Fabric

To print the doll face on cloth, you should have an ink jet copier/printer. I think that it is easier to make a paper copy of the face page rather than copying directly from the book to fabric.

- Cut a sheet of freezer paper 8½" by 11" (letter size).
  - I have found that Reynold's® brand freezer paper works better than house brands.
  - I have also used Sulky Sticky+ stabilizer paper in lieu of the freezer paper. This comes in rolls and sheets. The rolls are slightly narrower than 8½" but are wide enough for this use.
  - Another alternative I have tried is to spray a piece of 8½" by 11" (letter size) paper with quilt basting spray.
  - The patterns are narrow enough that you should be able to use A4 paper if that is more conveniently available than letter size paper. However, I have not tried this myself.
- Cut a piece of cotton doll making fabric that is slightly larger than the prepared freezer paper.
- The straight of grain should run down the length of the fabric. Note the straight of grain arrow in the middle of the Face Page.
- Make sure that the fabric is cut straight and is pressed flat.
- Lay the waxy side of the freezer paper on the wrong side of the fabric. In the other methods the sticky side of the paper also goes on the wrong side of the fabric. The 11" side of the paper should be lined up with the straight of grain. A small amount of fabric should show all around the paper.
- Iron the backing sheet to the fabric. Use the cotton setting of your iron. Press down on the fabric while you are ironing. Try to iron out all the air bubbles. Make sure that the fabric is stuck to the backing, especially at edges and corners.

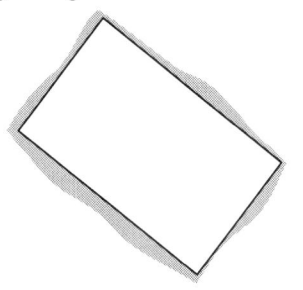

- Trim the fabric to the size of the paper.
- This step is optional. To help the prepared sheet pass smoothly through the printer, I like to fold a strip of masking tape across the end of the sheet that will to feed into the printer first. Fold the tape so that one half of the tape width is on the fabric side of the sheet and the other half of the tape width is on the paper side of the sheet. If you use tape, make sure that the tape is very flat and smooth. Do not leave creases or air pockets. After I smooth out the tape, I sometimes cover it with a pressing cloth and iron it.

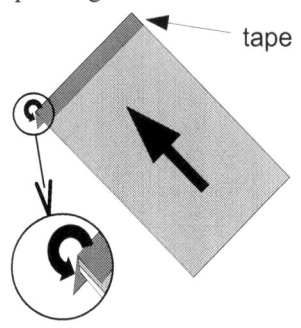

Printing the Face

- Place the prepared sheet in you copier so that the faces will be printed on the fabric side of the sheet.
- Copy the Face Page.
- Peel the tape and backing paper away from the fabric.
- Sometimes the paper backing can be used two or more times.

Completing the Face

- Use waterproof pens and pencils. Follow the directions: "Coloring the Face" below. On two faces on the Face Sheet the features are outlined in black. These outlines will show up clearly on dark skin tone fabric. The other faces have features that are outlined in gray. I have found that it is better to give faces printed in black ink black eye brows and lashes. Faces printed with gray ink can have black or brown brows and lashes.

Coloring the Face

1. Use your printed face outline or trace the face outline and features on fabric.
2. Color over brows and the top arch of the eye with brown or black pen. Fill in irises with blue or brown pencil. Fill in pupils with black pen. Outline irises with blue or brown pen to match pencil color. I have also made a green-eyed face by coloring the iris with green pencil and outlining the iris rim with green pen. Paint the whites of the eyes and eye reflections with white acrylic paint. Notice the placement of the reflection dots on the faces below. The pattern does not indicate the reflection dots' position. You may place them wherever you choose. Add nostril dots with brown pen. Outline nose shadows with orange pencil. Fill in lips with red pencil. Outline lips and lip part with red pen.

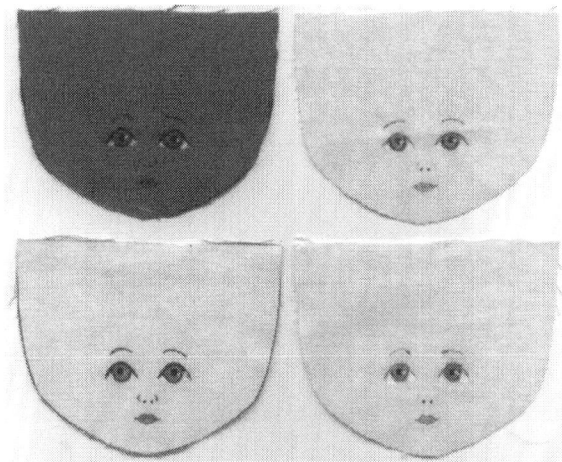

3. The four faces above were printed from a face page and then colored. Each face page has two faces with black feature outlines and four faces with gray feature outlines. The two faces on the left have their features outlined in black. The black ink faces show up much better than the gray ink faces on dark skin tone fabric.
4. Even if you are only planning to make one doll, you may want to color all six faces on the fabric Face Sheet. You can experiment with color and line width to find the combination that pleases you. For example, I made a doll with a suggestion of Asian features (she is wearing a green shirt on the front cover and playing the flute on the back) by giving my doll a wider upper eyelash and a straight lower lash.

Making the Head

1. Cut out the face and head back. Mark the darts on the wrong side of the head back and the inverted T on the right side of the head back. Sew in the darts. Stay stitch the face and head back ¼" (6 mm) from the top as indicated in the pattern. Right sides together hand baste the face and head back. Leave the top of the head open. When the sides are matched correctly, the head back will bow out slightly. Machine stitch. Trim the seam to ⅛" (3 mm). (Note that small sharp embroidery scissors are helpful when trimming and clipping seams.).

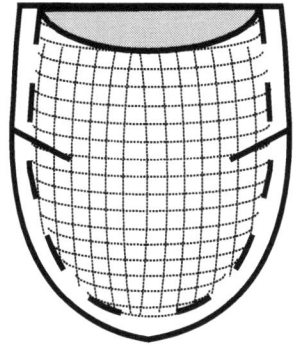

2. Turn the head right side out. Stuff firmly.
3. To close and round the top of the head turn the fabric under at the stay stitching. Gather this fabric by hand stitching into a circle. Secure the thread and sew around the stitching a second time for strength and to shrink the circle. When you have finished the circle should be about ½" (12 mm) in diameter.
4. If the gathered hole is still too large, sew around it a third time. Pull the thread as tightly as you can. Remove a little stuffing if necessary. The small hole at the top of the head will be covered by the embroidery floss hair.
5. Cut along the lines of the marked inverted T on the back of the head.

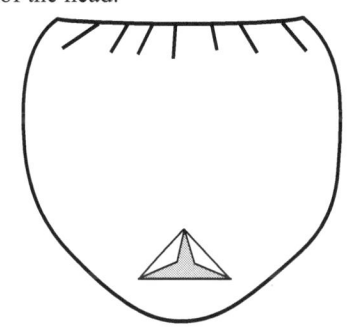

Squeeze a few drops of seam sealant onto a sheet of wax paper and use a toothpick to apply a very small amount of it to the cut edges. Allow the sealant to dry. Fold the cut corners inside the head to form a triangular opening.

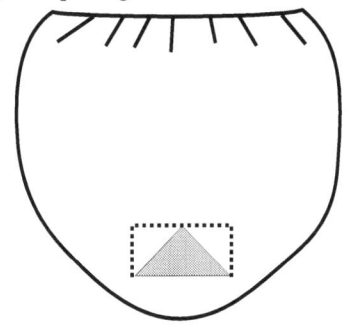

Add stuffing if needed to smooth the face and chin.

Body

Making Body Front and Back

1. Cut out body fronts and backs.
2. Mark dots to show stuffing opening on the wrong side of the body back. Mark the arm string and leg string lines on both the right and wrong side of all body pieces. Make certain that the string lines on the right side of the fabric are a little longer that ¼" (6 mm) so that they will still show up after the body has been sewn together.
3. With right sides together sew body front down the center front line using a ¼" (6 mm) seam.

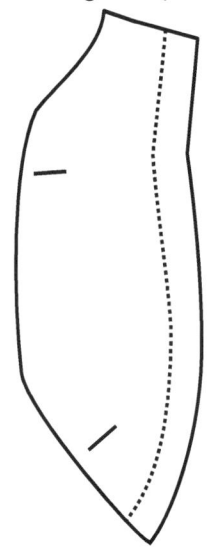

4. Finger press the seams open. (Note that I back stitch all the neck seams and the edges of the stuffing opening.)

5. With right sides together sew body backs together down the center back using a ¼" (6 mm) seam. Leave the space between the dots open for stuffing.

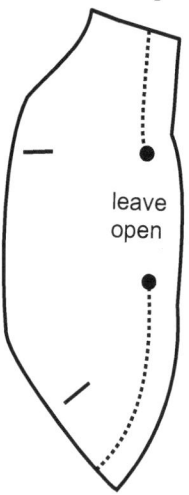

leave open

6. Finger press the seams and the unsewn area between them open.
7. For easier stuffing topstitch around the opening in the center back.

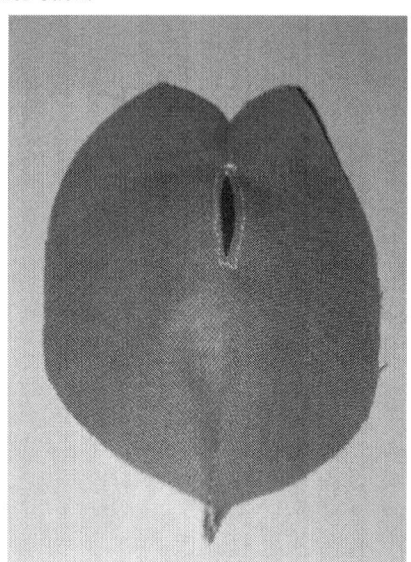

Assembling Body

1. With right sides together pin and baste the body front to the body back. Match the front and back string lines. The edges will meet, but the pieces will not lie flat.
2. Sew all the way around the body using a ¼" (6 mm) seam.
3. Leave the neck open. Clip curves. Turn right side out. (Note that a hemostat makes turning much easier.)

4. Place a cylindrical object through the back opening and into neck to keep the neck open.

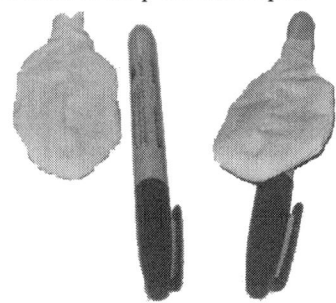

5. Squeeze a few drops of seam sealant onto a sheet of wax paper and use a toothpick to put a very small amount of the sealant around the neck opening. Allow the sealant to dry.

Attaching Head and Body

1. Leave the cylindrical object in the neck to keep it open while sewing. Insert the neck into the prepared opening in the back of the head. Position the head correctly on the body. The nose and mouth should be lined up with the body center front.

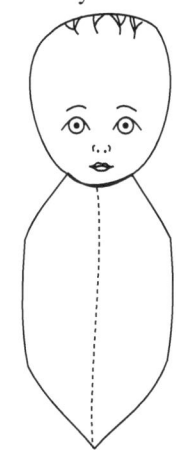

2. To stitch the head to the neck using the ladder stitch take one tiny stitch in the head. Take the next tiny stitch in the neck. Take the third stitch in the head as close as possible to the first stitch. Alternate stitches between the head and neck until you have completely sewn the head to the body. I have written more about the ladder stitch in **Tips** (p 64).
3. Remove the cylindrical object from the neck and stuff the body firmly. Close the back with an overcasting stitch. I have written more about the overcasting stitch in **Tips** (p 64).

Arms and Legs

Marking and Sewing Arms and Legs

1. Using a peach pencil or air soluble pen trace two arms and two legs on wrong side of folded fabric. Mark the spaces to be left open . The peach pencil works on both light and dark fabric.

2. Use an open embroidery foot to sew on traced lines. I like to place my Ott-lite on my machine table to my left to help me see the lines. If you have a needle down option on your machine, it is helpful for this type of sewing. Do not sew on areas of templates marked leave open, including the toe space on the foot.

Cutting and Beginning to Stuff Arms and Legs

1. Cut out the sewn limbs. Leave a ⅛" (3 mm) allowance in most areas. Leave a ¼" (6 mm) allowance around arm and leg openings. Leave a ¼" (6 mm) allowance at the top and bottom of the foot. The larger seam allowance makes it easier to match the foot seams.

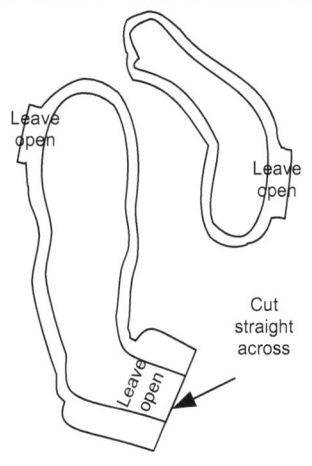

2. Finger press the seams of the top and bottom of the foot open. Bring the top and bottom of each foot together. Match the seams carefully. Sew across the foot using a ¼" (6 mm) seam.

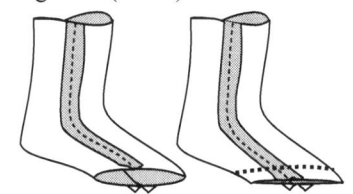

3. Turn the arms and legs right side out. I find a hemostat is very helpful for this step.
4. Begin stuffing the arms and legs firmly. Stop at the stuffing openings.

Marking the Finger Lines

1. For optional fingers, mark finger lines with an air soluble pen on the top and palm of each hand.
2. Make sure to aline the finger lines on the top of the hand with the finger lines on the palm of the hand.

Sewing the First Finger

1. Sew the fingers by hand. Thread a needle and tie a small knot at the end of the thread. Start at the inside of one finger line on the palm. You will be sewing toward the finger tip.

2. Push the needle all the way through the palm. Bring the needle out at the same point on the finger line at the top of the hand.

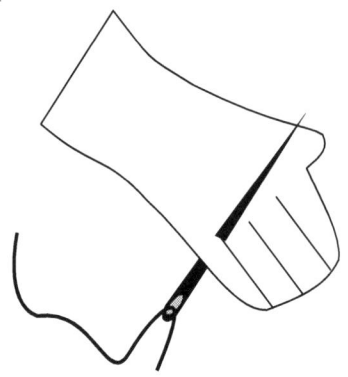

3. Gently pull the thread until the knot goes inside the palm, but does not go all the way through the hand.
4. Make tiny stitches one at a time by moving the needle back and forth through the hand. Always stitch on the finger line.

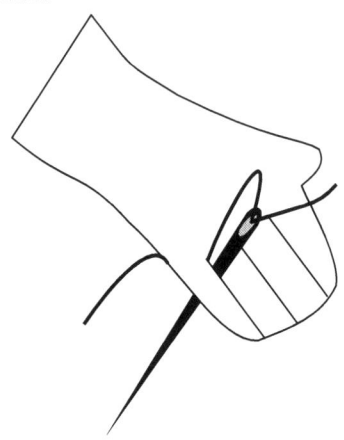

Moving Between Finger Lines

1. When you reach the tip of the finger send the needle through the hand without catching any fabric to the tip of the next finger line.

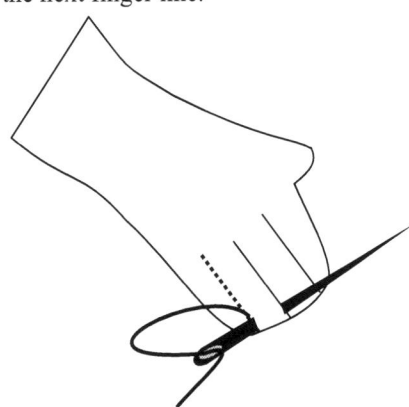

2. Sew the next finger line in the same manner as the first finger line. This time start at the finger tip and sew toward the wrist.
3. When you reach the bottom of the finger line, push the needle through the inside of the hand to the bottom of the last finger line.

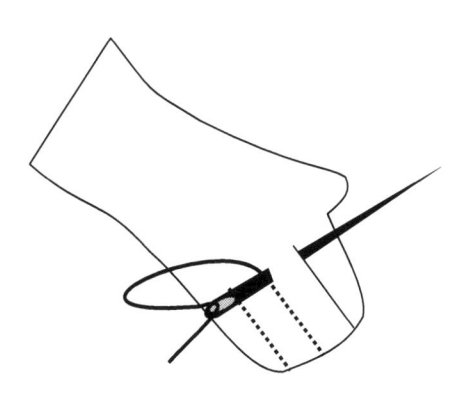

Finishing the Last Finger Line

1. Sew the last finger line. At the tip of the finger go around the last stitch with the needle several times to secure the thread.
2. To hide the thread end send the needle and thread back through the hand without catching any fabric on either side of the hand.
3. Bring the needle out through the top of the hand.

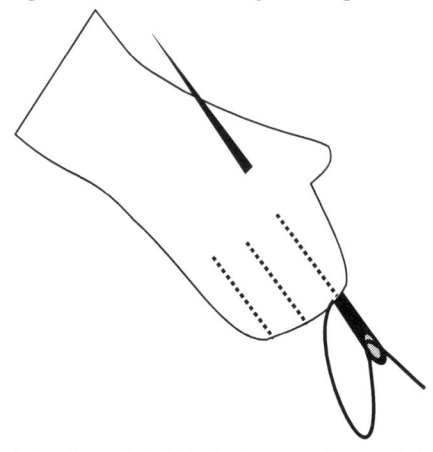

4. Pull the thread tightly before cutting and clip the thread close to the fabric. When the thread is released, the end of the thread will go back inside the hand and be hidden. The toes will be made after the limbs are attached to the body.

Positioning the Arms and Legs

1. Lay the doll body with attached head on a table.

2. Lay the arms and legs on the table so that the parts of the arms and legs that will be touching the body are facing up.

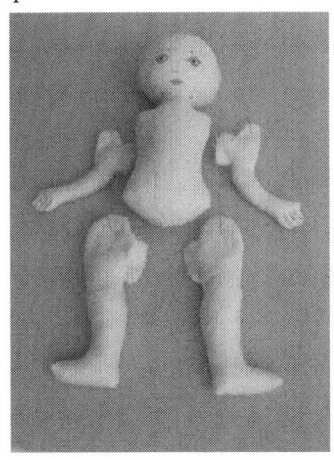

Gluing Stringing Buttons Inside Arms and Legs

1. Use ½" (12 mm) diameter arm buttons.
2. Use fabric glue stick to glue a button inside each arm where the arm will touch the doll's body. Line the button eyes up with the dots indicated on the templates. Make sure that the doll has a left and right arm. Do not tuck the seam allowances of the stuffing openings in until you have finished stringing the doll. (See photo above.) Stick a pin through each button eye while the glue is drying. The pin will show if the eyes are in the correct position. They will also leave small holes in the fabric that will be helpful during the stringing.

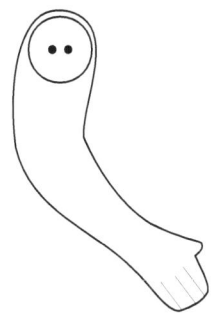

3. Follow the same instructions for gluing the buttons inside the legs. Use ⅝" (16 mm) diameter buttons.

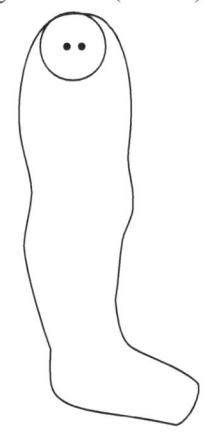

4. Allow the glue to dry.

Stringing the Arms and Legs

Inserting the String into the First Arm

1. Cut a 36" (91 cm) length of unwaxed dental floss. Fold it in half to make a 18" (45 cm) length of floss. Use a needle threader to thread a 2¼" (5 cm) or longer needle with the doubled length of floss.
2. Carefully insert the needle into the opening of one arm. Push the needle through button eye A and out the arm.

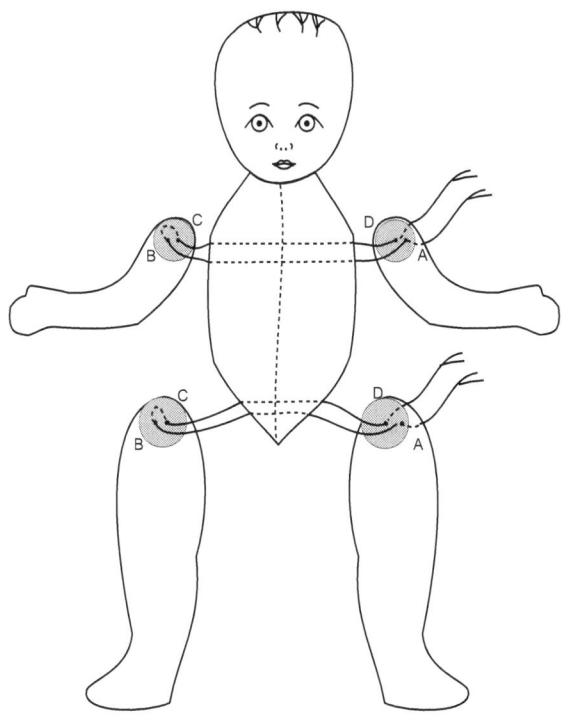

3. Gently pull most of the floss out of the arm. Leave a 3" (7 cm) tail of floss outside the arm. Do not pull the floss tightly. Rest the doll's body and arms on a table while you are working to keep the floss from pulling out of the arm. I usually stand while I am stringing dolls.

Sending the String through the Body Front

1. Insert the needle through the arm string line at the body front.
2. Push the needle all the way through the body front and come out at the second arm string line on the body front.

Looping the String through the Second Arm

1. Insert the needle through the second arm and into button eye B. Carefully bring the needle out of the stuffing opening without catching any fabric.
2. Reinsert the needle into the stuffing opening and insert it into button eye C.

Sending the string through the Body Back

1. Pull the needle out of the arm and insert it into the arm string line on the body back.
2. Push the needle all the way through the body back and come out the second body back arm string line.
3. Push the needle into the first arm through button eye D.

Tying off the Stringing Floss

1. Carefully bring the needle out of the arm through the stuffing opening. Do not catch any extra fabric with the needle.
2. Unthread the needle. Pull the 3" (7 cm) of floss left outside the first arm and unthreaded end of the floss together until the arms are in the correct position on the body.
3. Tie a square knot with the floss and then a second square knot.
4. Cut the floss about 1" (2.5 cm) from the end of the knots.

Finishing Stuffing

1. Tuck the seam allowances for the stuffing openings and the floss ends into the arm.
2. Stuff around the floss. Finish stuffing arms and close with ladder stitch or overcasting stitch.
3. Attach the legs in the same manner as the arms.
4. Add toes if you like.

Toes

Preparing to Define the Toes

1. Mark the toes on the top and sole of each foot with an air soluble pen. Make sure to aline the toe lines on the top of the foot with the toe lines on the sole of the foot.

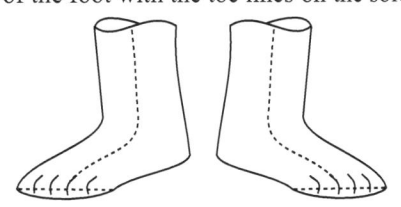

2. Thread a needle and tie a small knot at one end. I use tan thread on a doll with peach skin to make the toes more visible.

Beginning the Sewing

1. Start from the sole of the foot. Put the needle in the foot at the end of the big toe line.
2. Bring the needle out at the top of the foot at the same point on the big toe line.

3. Pull the thread all the way through the foot and gently tug until the knot is inside the foot.

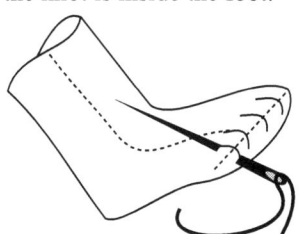

Defining the Toes

1. Insert the needle back in the hole on the sole of the foot where you began making the toe and push it through the line on the top of the foot for the second toe. The thread should have wrapped around the edge of the foot to define the big toe.

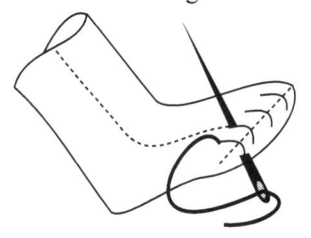

2. Follow the diagram to finish defining the toes.

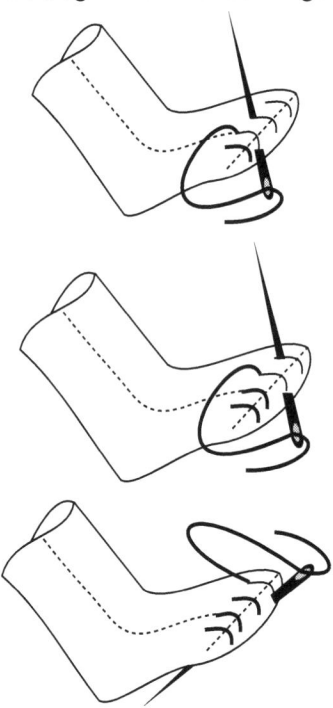

Securing the Thread

1. After you have defined the little toe, take several tiny stitches in the sole at the inside edge of the little toe line to secure the thread.
2. To hide the thread end send the needle and thread back through the last hole in the foot without catching any fabric on either side of the foot. Bring the needle out through the middle of the sole. Pull the thread tightly before cutting it close to the fabric. When the thread is

released, the end of the thread will go back inside the foot and be hidden.

Hair

Cutting and Sewing the Bangs

1. Cut one bangs guide and one braid guide from tear-away stabilizer. Mark the sew lines and floss lines.
2. Take one skein of embroidery floss and cut it into quarters. 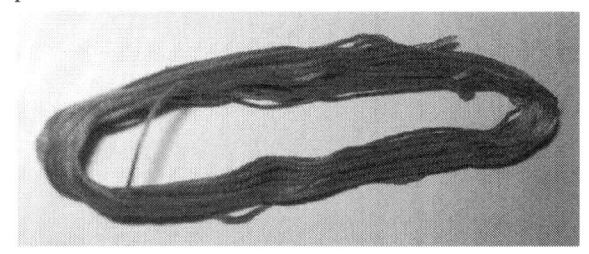 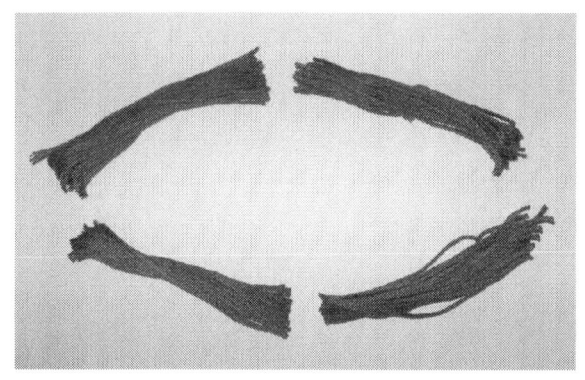
3. The individual strands of floss will be slightly over 3" (7 cm) each. Arrange them on the tear-away stabilizer marked for bangs. 
4. Sew the floss on your machine with matching thread where indicated on the stabilizer..
5. Use a toothbrush, doll brush, or fine comb to separate the strands of embroidery floss. Remove the stabilizer

Attaching the Bangs to the Head

1. Pull out about 24" (60 cm) of floss from one of the remaining skeins of embroidery floss. Separate two strands from this length. Use the separated strands to sew the bangs to the head by hand.
2. The bangs floss should cover the forehead above the eyebrows. The floss behind the bangs should cover the top and back of the head including the hole surrounded by gathering stitches. This back hair will be covered by the floss that will be parted to make braids. 
3. Pin bangs to head and hand sew along the seam line.
4. Use fabric glue to hold the floss to the top and back of the head. Use a small amount of glue under the bangs at the top of the forehead. Leave most of the bang floss loose.
5. Carefully trim any floss at the back of the head that does not lie neatly.

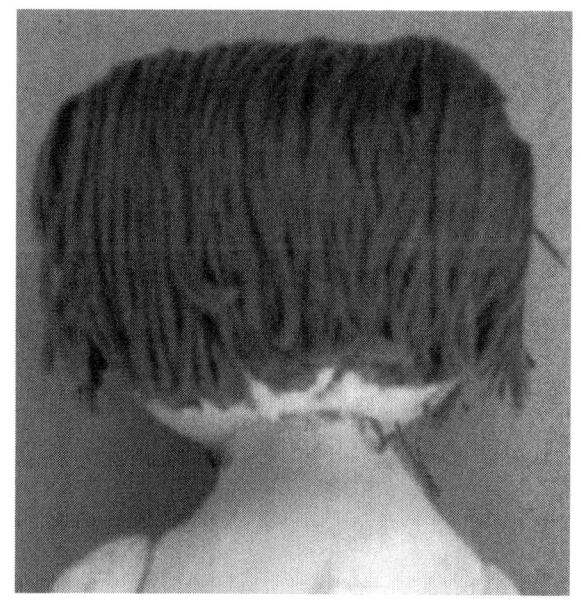

Cutting and Sewing the Part

1. Use 4 skeins of floss.
2. Cut each skein in half. 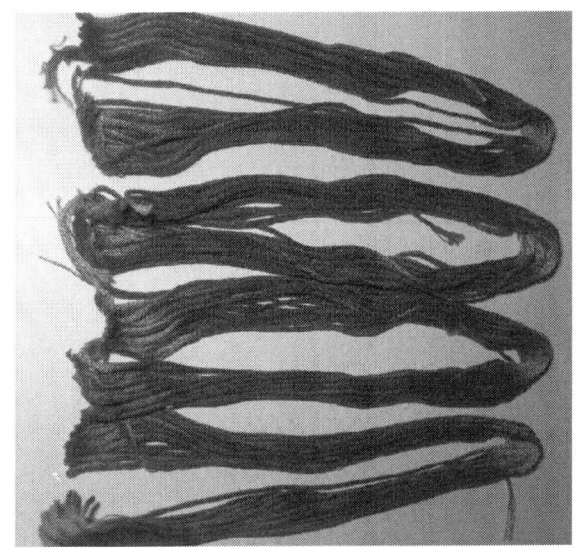
3. Place the braid tear-away stabilizer under the middle of the floss. Each strand of floss is about 12" (30 cm) long. Arrange the floss on the stabilizer so that the middle fold of the floss is on the sew line of the stabilizer.
4. Sew through the middle of the floss so that there is about 6" (15 cm) of floss on each side of the machine stitching. 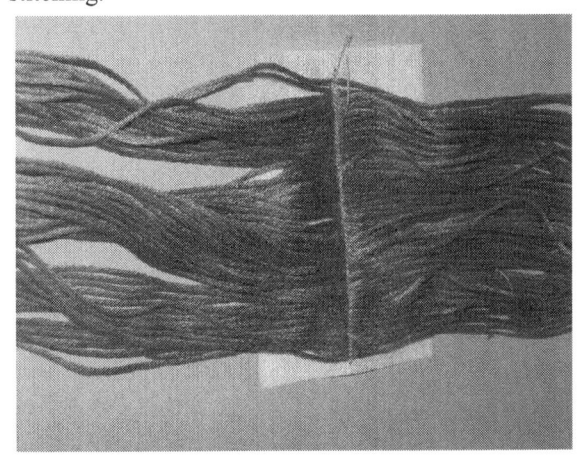
5. Use a toothbrush, doll brush, or fine comb to separate the strands of embroidery floss. Remove the stabilizer

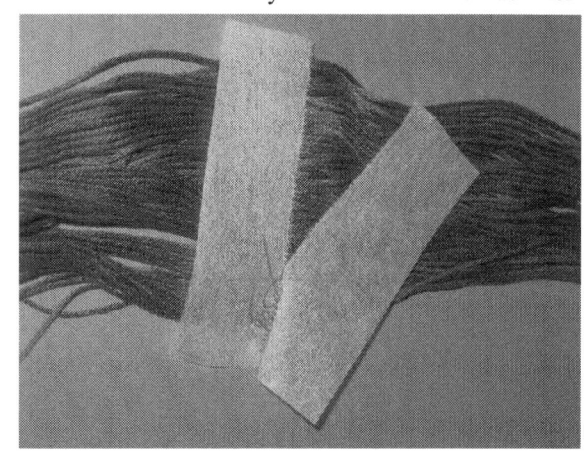

Attaching the Part to the Head

1. Arrange the floss so that the bangs seam is hidden and the part runs down the middle of the head.
2. Pin in place. Use two strands of the reserved floss to sew the part in place.

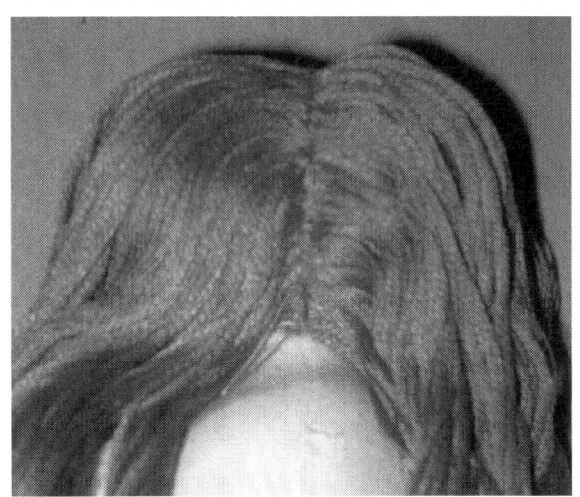

Making the Braids

1. Make a pony tail on each side of the head. Use the last two strands of reserved floss to sew each pony tail to the head.

2. Braid each pony tail and secure with the rest of the floss.

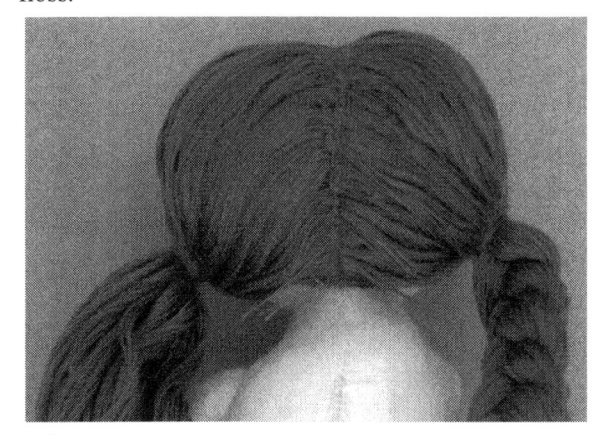

3. Trim the floss below the braid ties as needed.

Adding Blush

If you would like pink cheeks on your doll, add powdered blush on the finished doll. Put a small amount of blush on each cheek with a small brush or cotton swab. Rub the color in with a makeup sponge or dry wash cloth.

Panties

1. Cut out two panties
2. Lay the lace on the right side of the fabric at the leg opening. The lace heading should overlap the raw edge. The lace should extend below the knit fabric.

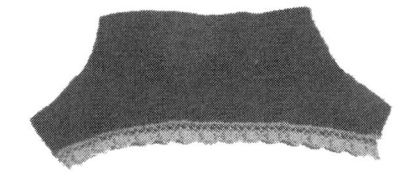

3. Use a narrow zigzag seam to sew a lace edging on each of the two fabric pieces at leg openings (A-A and at B-B).

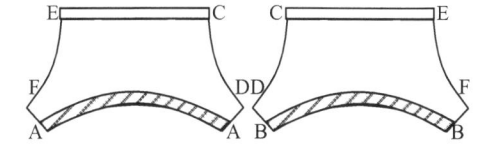

4. Lay elastic on the wrong side of each pantie leg. Anchor the elastic at one end of leg opening. Use a wide zigzag to sew on either side of the elastic. Do not catch the elastic with the needle. Pull the elastic through the zigzag stitching until it measures about 2½" (12 mm). Secure the second end of the elastic and cut off excess elastic.
5. With right sides together match the double notches and sew the two pieces together at C-D in the center front of the panties.
6. Sew the seam with a zigzag stitch. Do not sew center back yet. (Note the ⅛" (3 mm) seam for knits.)

7. Make an elastic casing by folding ¼" (6 mm) of fabric under at the waist (E-C-E.) Sew the raw edge of the casing with a narrow zigzag stitch to finish the edge while making the casing.

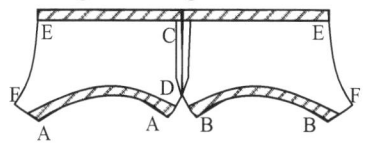

8. Insert elastic in the waist casing. Secure at one end. Pull the elastic in the casing without stretching the elastic to about 4½" (11cm).
9. Secure the second end of the elastic and cut off excess elastic.
10. With right sides together sew center back at E-F matching the triple notches.
11. Finish seam.

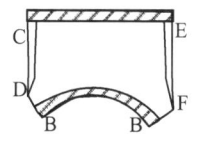

12. Fold panties so that the center front C and center back E are touching and edges of the insides of the legs are together and ready to be sewn.
13. Sew leg seams at A-D-B.
14. Finish seam.

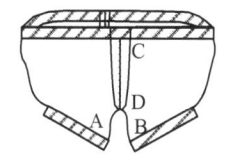

15. Turn right side out

Camisole

1. Cut out camisole. Mark the A and B dots on the wrong side of the fabric.
2. Lay a strip of lace on the right side of the fabric at the top of the camisole. The heading of the lace should be touching the raw edge at the top of the camisole. The edge of the lace should be inside the camisole.
3. Use a narrow zigzag seam. Sew lace without gathering around the top of the camisole.
4. Lay a strip of lace on the right side of the fabric at the bottom of the camisole. The heading of the lace should be touching the raw edge at the bottom of the camisole. The edge of the lace should be inside the camisole.
5. Use a narrow zigzag seam to sew lace edging to the bottom of the camisole.

6. Press under ½" (12 mm) of fabric on each side of the center back. Try on doll. The openings should come together at the center back.

15

7. Sew hook and loop tape to the back of the camisole. Instructions for sewing hook and loop tape are in **Tips** (p 69).
8. Mark dots A and B on both sides of garment with air soluble pen.
9. Cut two 2½" (6 cm) lengths of ribbon.
10. On the inside of the garment hand sew each piece of ribbon to the front of the garment where the A dots have been marked.
11. Pin the ribbon lengths to the back of the garment where the B dots have been marked. Leave about 1" (2.5 cm) of ribbon between the A and B dots to serve as shoulder straps.

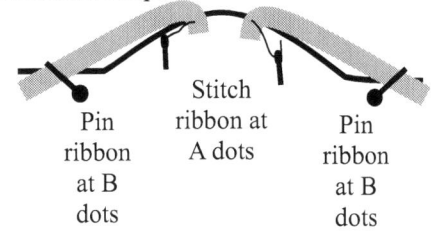

Pin ribbon at B dots — Stitch ribbon at A dots — Pin ribbon at B dots

12. Try the garment on the doll and adjust the straps.
13. Hand sew the pinned ribbon lengths to the back of the garment.
14. Sew an applique on front of camisole if desired.

Sandals

1. Cut out two soles and two insoles from felt.
2. Mark the line guide on the insoles.
3. Cut two 1¼" (3 cm) insteps from ¼" (6 mm) ribbon.
4. To make the insole band for each sandal, line up the ribbon with the guide line. The ribbon makes a loop with the two raw edges touching.
5. Cut 1½" (3 cm) narrow ribbon for each sandal heel.
6. Fold the heel ribbon in half and glue the raw edges under the heel of each insole. Leave about ½" (12 mm) of ribbon sticking out of the insole.
7. Glue the insole to the sole with the raw edges of the ribbons sandwiched between the two soles

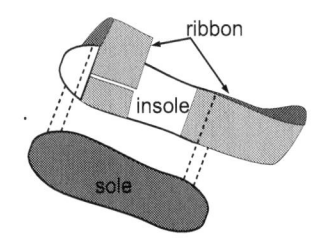

8. Use miniature clothes pins to hold the sole in place while the glue dries.
9. Thread a 10" (25 cm) long ⅛" (3 mm) wide ribbon through the ribbon loop at the sandal heel. Tack the ribbon in place with a few hand stitches.
10. Put the sandal on the doll and tie at the ankle.

Face Page

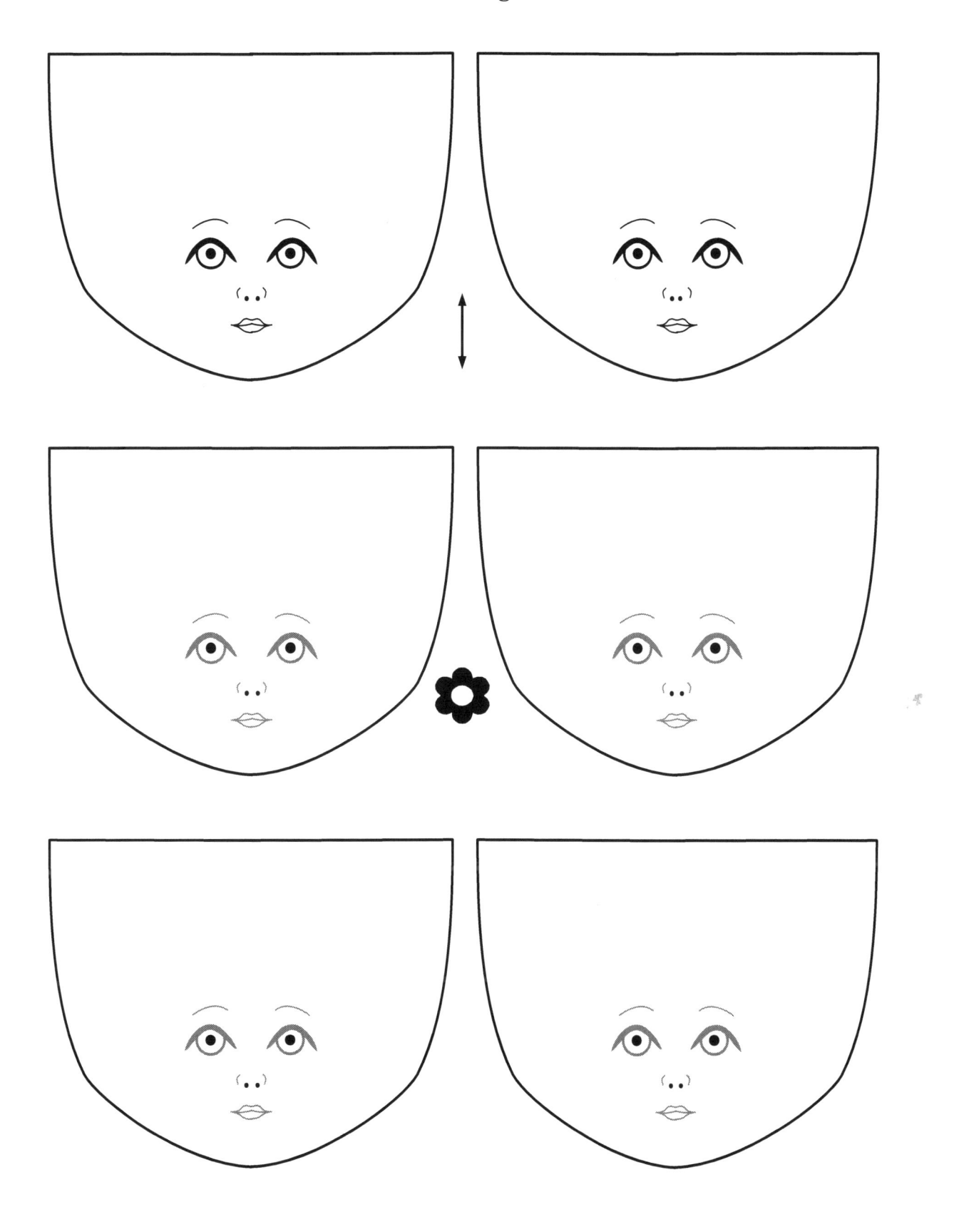

17

Florabunda Doll

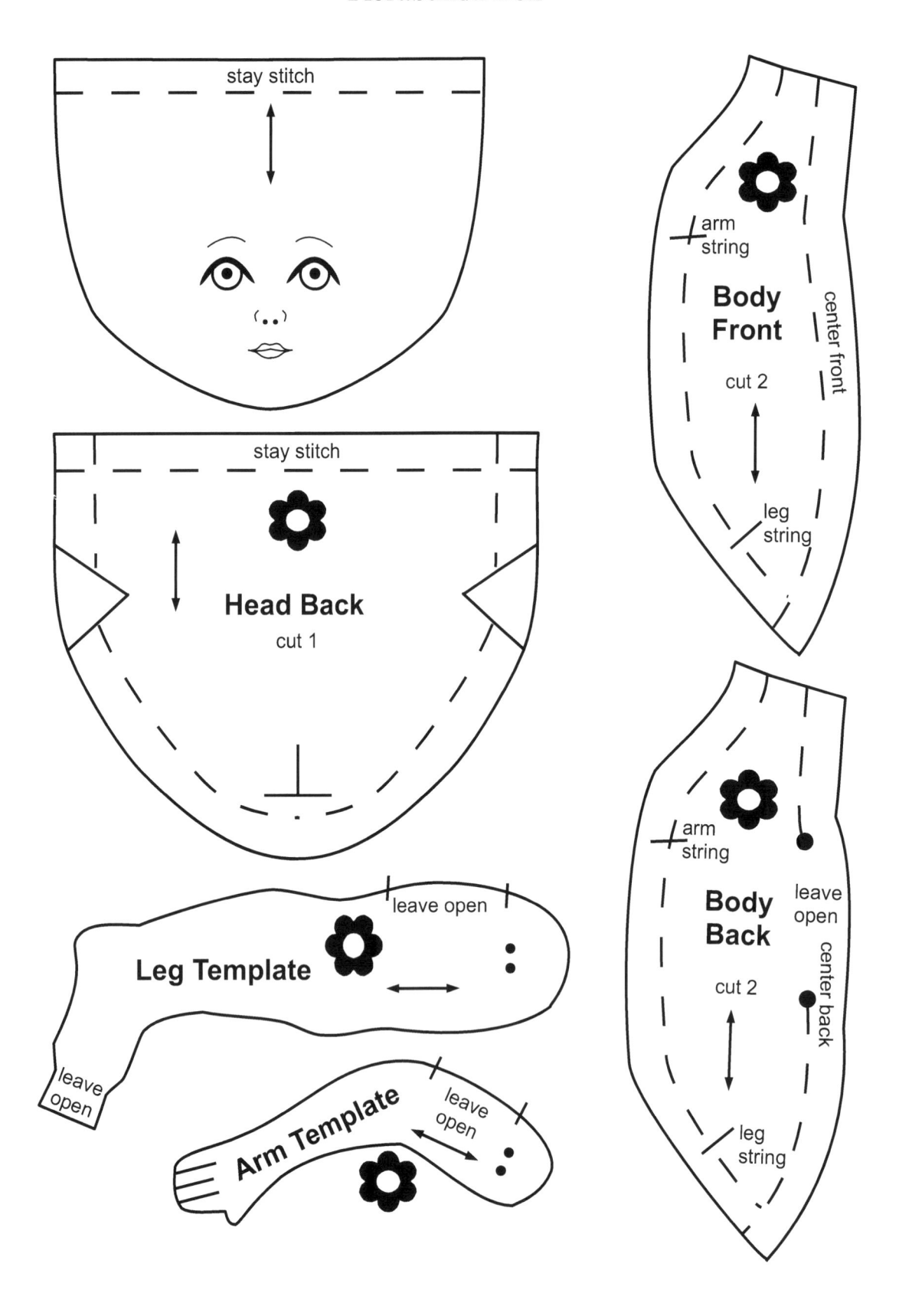

18

Florabunda Doll

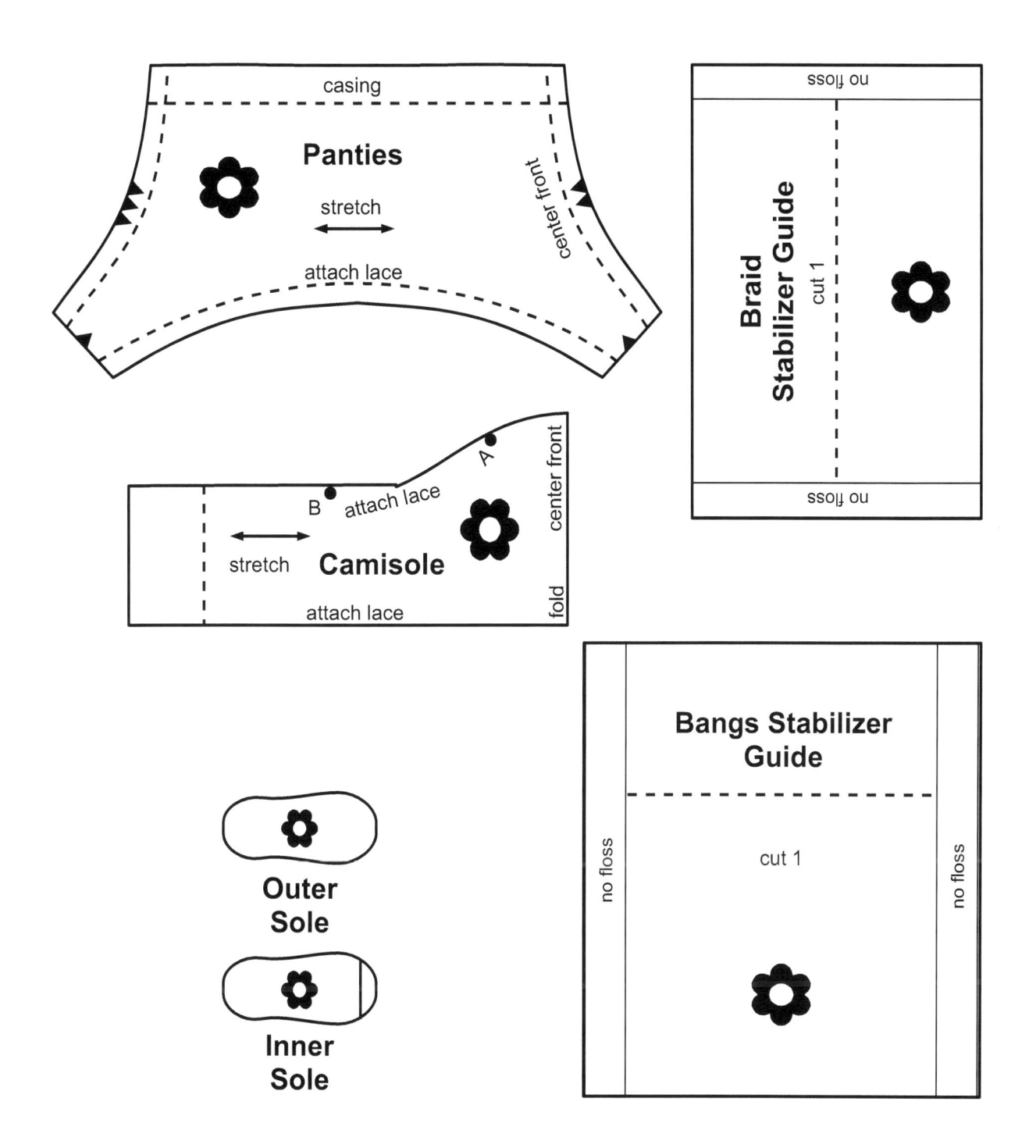

Sewing a Small Doll and Her Clothing
www.sherralynsdolls.com

Gown, Smock Top, and Two Tier Skirt

Supplies

- Scraps of soft cotton fabric with soft colors or small prints (The gown may be made in cotton flannel.)
- Matching thread
- Narrow ribbon (Gown)
- ⅛" (3 mm) elastic
- Optional fairly thin lady's sock for sleep cap
- Optional 1.3 cm pompom for sleep cap

Equipment

- Basic sewing tools (see **Tools, Tips, and Techniques**)

Skills

- Gown and Smock Top
    - Use **Tools, Tips, and Techniques** for instructions on applying hook and loop tape.
- Two Tiered Skirt
    - Joining gathered fabric to ungathered fabric

Sizes

- Florabunda's (✿) Clothing Patterns Fit
    - Sherralyn's Dolls' Florabunda
    - Madam Alexander's® 7½" (19 cm) Wendy
    - Vogue Doll Company's® Modern and Vintage Ginny®
    - Lillian Vernon's® 7½" (19 cm) doll

Introduction

These instructions describe the construction of a gown, smock, and two tiered skirt for Florabunda and other 7½" to 8" (19 to 20 cm) dolls.

Symbols

- The pattern pieces for Florabunda's clothing are marked by a flower (✿).
- In the patterns a thick broken line indicates where to gather the fabric.
- In these instructions light gray indicates the right side of the fabric

Gown and Smock Top

Cutting and Marking

- Cut one smock or gown front on the fold and two backs.
- Mark the notches.

Sewing Shoulder/Sleeve Seams

- Match the single notches at the shoulder seam/sleeve top. Sew shoulder seams and finish the seams.
- Press the finished seam to the back of the garment.
- Finish the raw edges of sleeves, neck, and back closings.
- Press the back closings ½" (12 mm) to the inside and then the neck edge ¼" (6 mm) to the inside. The top edges of the back opening will be folded to the inside along with the rest of the neck edge.

Hand Gathering the Neck

- Start at the center back. Hand gather the neck. Sew near the neck opening and catch all the fabric layers that have been pressed to the inside of the garment. Gather the neck to 3½".

Sewing Elastic Casing In Sleeves

- To make each sleeve casing press the finished casing edge ½" (12 mm) to the inside. Topstitch ¼" to ⅜" (6 to 9 mm) from the edge.

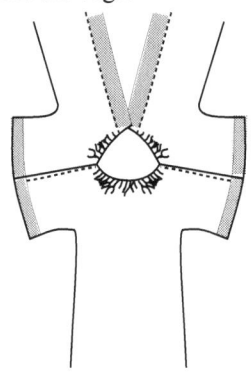

- Insert elastic into the casing and anchor one end of the elastic by sewing it down at one casing opening.
- Gather the casing fabric over the elastic without stretching the elastic to about 2" (5 cm).
- Check the fit around the wrist on the doll.
- Secure the second side of the elastic to the second casing opening by sewing through it and the casing several times.
- Cut off the excess elastic.

Sides, Back, and Hem

- Fold right sides together at the shoulder seams and match the double notches at the garment's sides. Sew across the bottom of each sleeve and down the garment's side. Finish the seams.

- Either garment opens all the way down the back. Close the back with hook and loop tape. The instructions are in **Tips** (p 69).
- Finish the raw edge of the hem.
- Press a ½" (12 mm) hem in the gown, or a ¼" (6 mm) hem in the top and topstitch or whip in the hem.

Two Tier Skirt

Cutting and Marking

- Cut one skirt top tier and one skirt bottom tier on the fold.
- Mark notches and the center front and back.

Joining the Gathered Tier to the Top Tier

- Run two parallel lines of gathering stitches where indicated on skirt bottom tier.

- Pull up the gathering stitches to match the skirt top tier. Match the notches and the center front.
- Pin or baste the two tiers and sew them together.

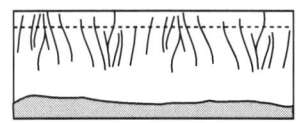

- Finish the seam.

Sewing Elastic Casing in Skirt

- Finish the raw edges at the top and bottom of the skirt.
- To make casing at the skirt's waist press the finished casing edge ½" (12 mm) to the inside.
- Topstitch ¼" to ⅜" (6 to 9 mm) from the edge.

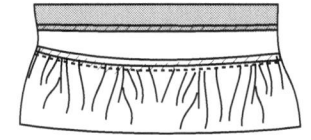

- Insert elastic into the casing and anchor one end of the elastic by sewing it down at one casing opening.
- Gather the casing fabric over the elastic without stretching the elastic to about 5¾" (14 cm).
- Check the fit on the doll's waist and secure the second side of the elastic by sewing through it and the casing several times

Finishing the Skirt

- Sew the back closing and finish the seam.
- Press the hem ¼" (6 mm) to the inside. Slip-stitch or topstitch the hem.

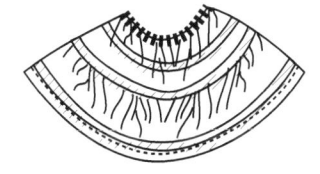

Stocking Sleep Cap

This sleep cap is an easy and enjoyable project.

- Measure down from the top of the sock about 6" (15 cm).

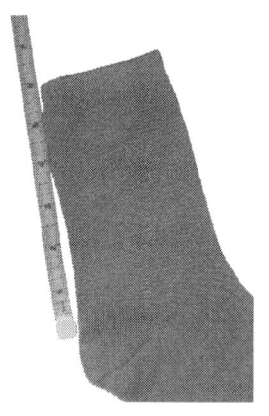

- Cut across the sock to make two pieces: a tube and a piece containing the heel and toe.

- Use the heel and toe of the sock for another project. The sleep cap will be made from the tube.
- Turn the tube wrong side out.
- Hand gather all the way around the cut edge of the tube.
- Pull the gathers until the raw edge of the tube is completely closed to make a cap. I like to go over the gathering several times and secure the thread each time. I think that effort gives the hand sewing more strength.

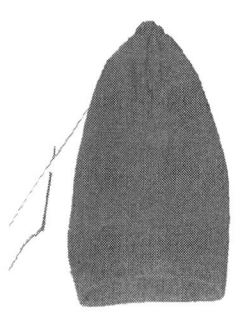

- Turn the cap right side out.

- Sew or glue a pompom over the gathered end.

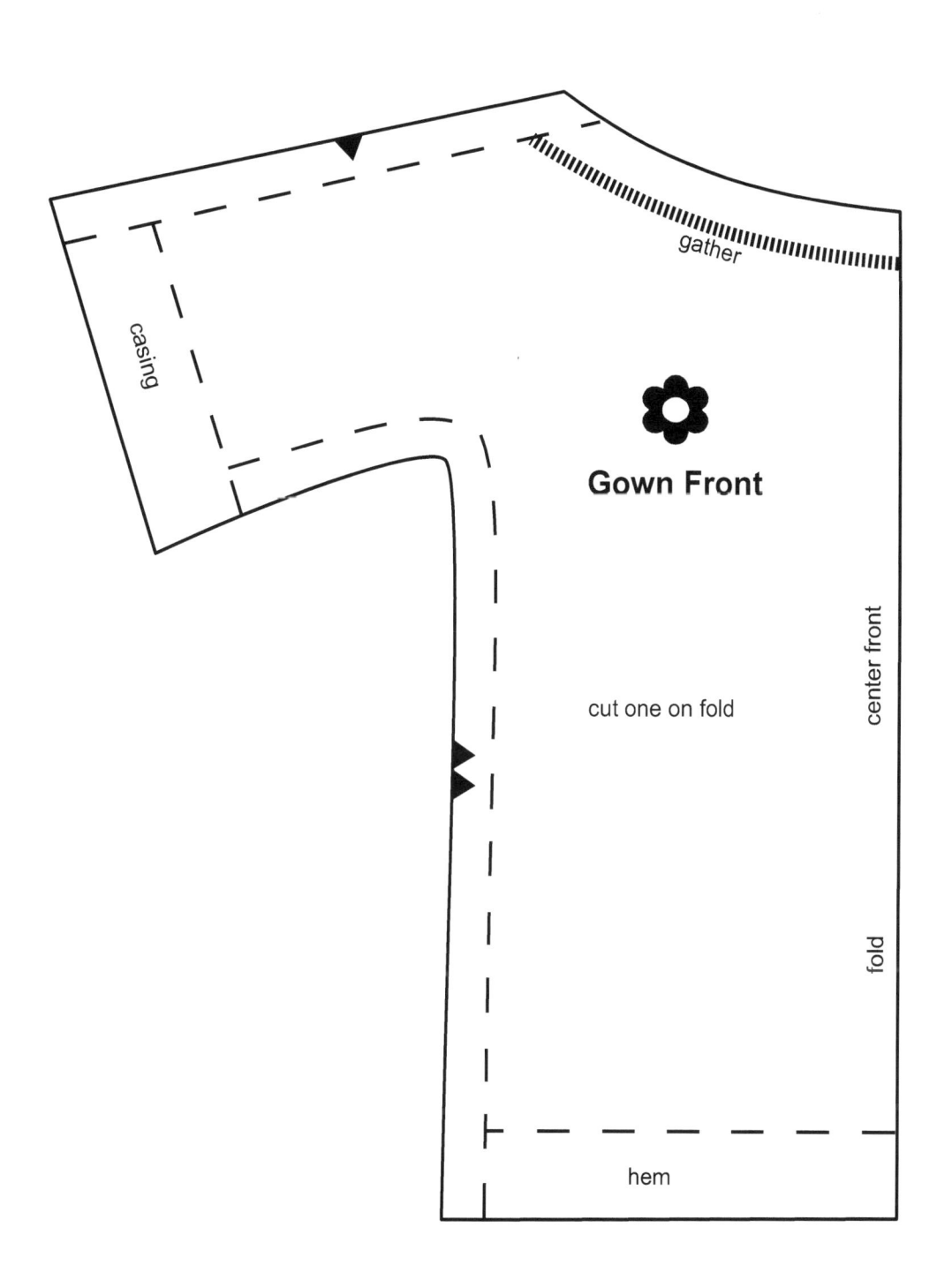

Gown, Smock Top, and Two Tier Skirt

Gown Front

cut one on fold

casing
gather
center front
fold
hem

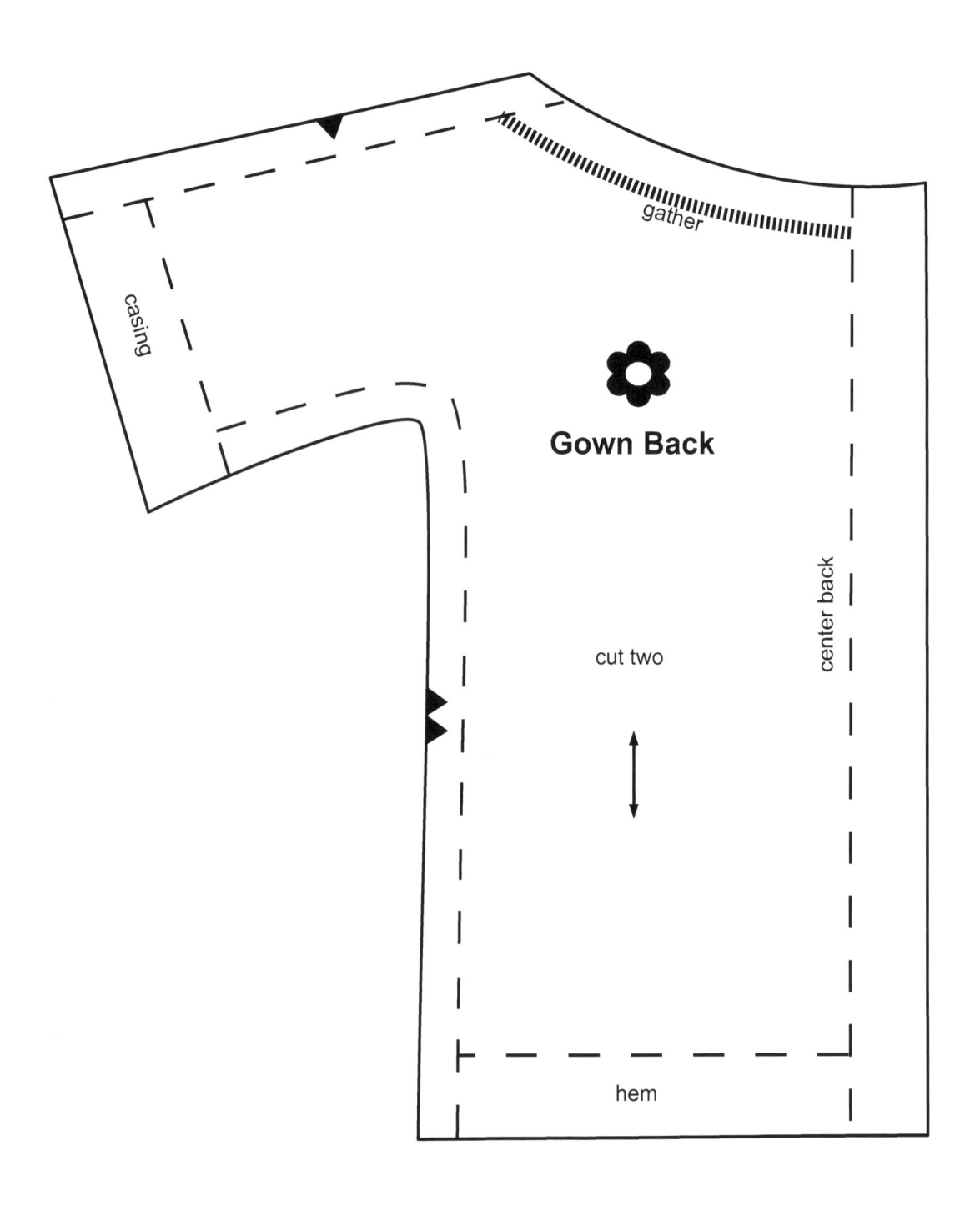

Gown, Smock Top, and Two Tier Skirt

Gown Back

casing

gather

center back

cut two

hem

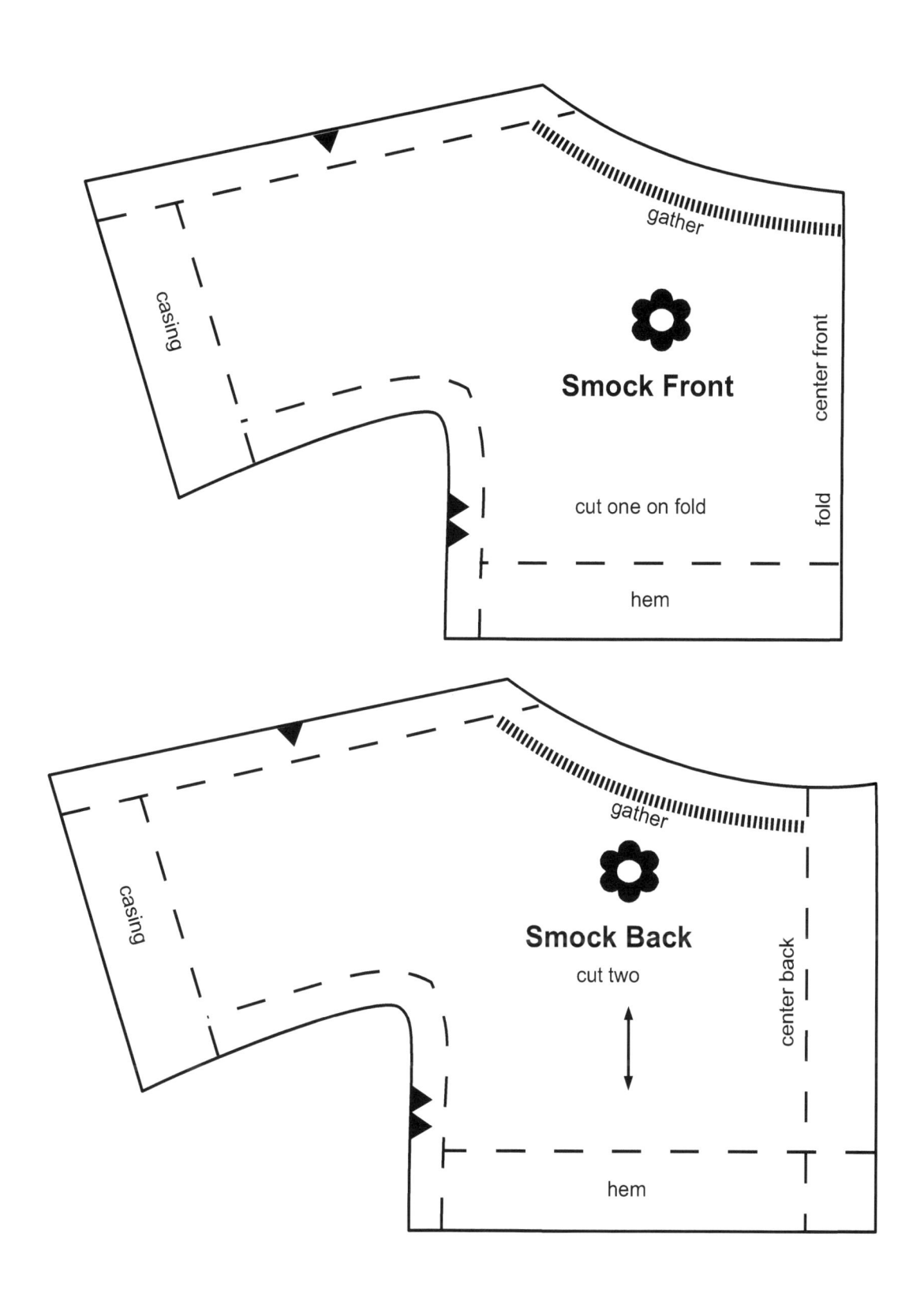

Gown, Smock Top, and Two Tier Skirt

27

Gown, Smock Top, and Two Tier Skirt

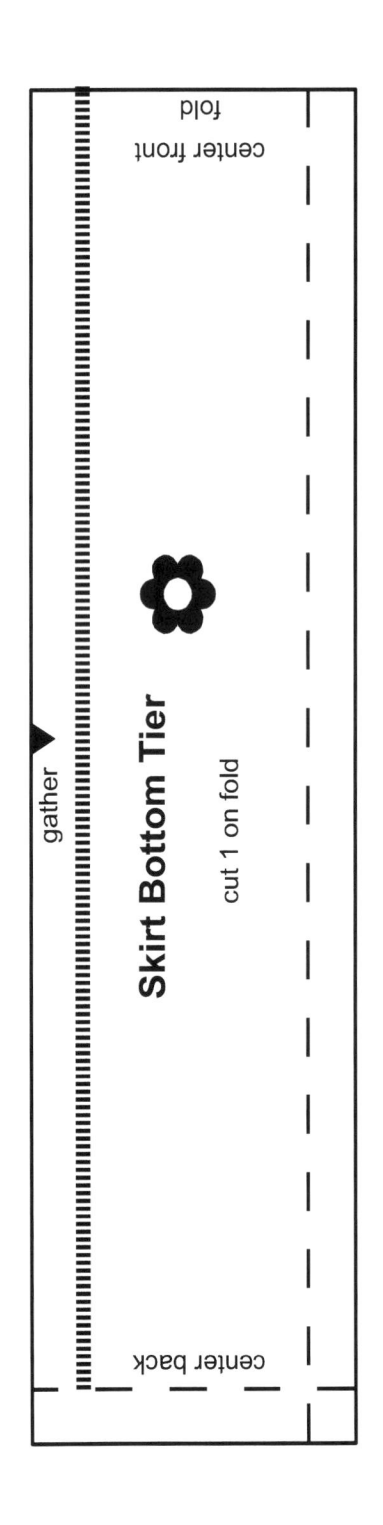

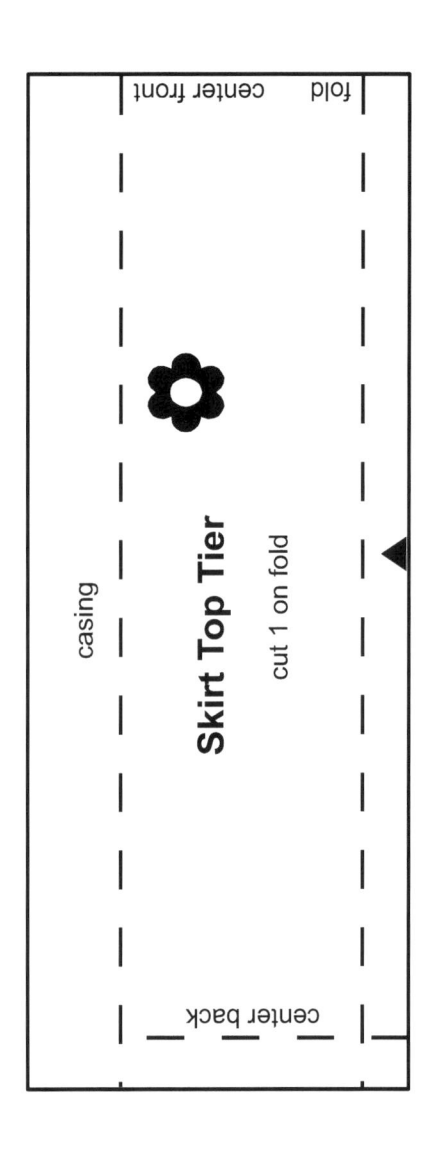

28

Sewing a Small Doll and Her Clothing
www.sherralynsdolls.com

A-line Dress with Short Jacket and Bloomer

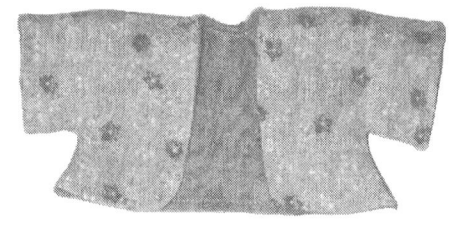

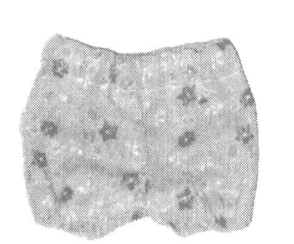

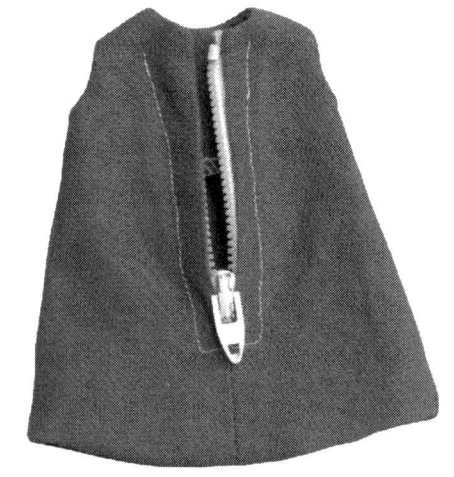

Supplies

- Light cotton fabric in soft colors or small prints (dress)
- Light cotton fabric to match or compliment A-line dress (jacket and bloomers)
- Matching thread
- Hook and loop tape for closing back (unless you plan to close the dress with a zipper)
- 2" (5 cm) nylon zipper (optional for closing dress back instead of hook and loop tape)
- Optional small buttons or appliques
- ⅛" (3 mm) elastic (bloomers)

Equipment

- Basic sewing tools (see **Tools, Tips, and Techniques**)
- Hemostat to turn dress and facing

Skills

- Dress
  - Applying a facing to both neck opening and armholes (explained in the instructions)
  - Use **Tools, Tips, and Techniques** for instructions on applying hook and loop tape.
  - Applying a zipper to the back opening (optional)
- Jacket
  - Lining a jacket

Sizes

- Florabunda's (❋) Clothing Patterns Fit
  - Sherralyn's Dolls' Florabunda
  - Madam Alexander's® 7½" (19 cm) Wendy
  - Vogue Doll Company's® Modern and Vintage Ginny®
  - Lillian Vernon's® 7½" (19 cm) doll

Introduction

These instructions describe the construction of an A-line dress, jacket, and bloomers for Florabunda and other 7½" to 8" (19 to 20 cm) dolls.

Symbols

- The pattern pieces for Florabunda's clothing are marked by a flower (✿).
- In these instructions light gray indicates the right side of the fabric

A-line Dress

Cutting and Marking

- Cut one front and one front facing on fold. Cut two backs and two back facings.
- Mark the notches.

Applying Facing

- Match the single notches. Sew dress front to dress backs at shoulders.
- Press seams open.
- Match the single notches. Sew facing front to facing back at shoulders.
- Press seams open.
- Finish bottom of front and back facings.
- Right sides together lay facing on the dress matching neck, armholes, and back openings.
- Sew all the way around the neck and then around each armhole. 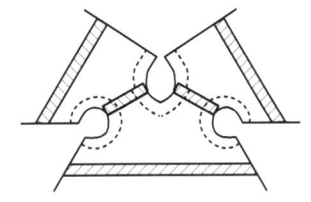
- Trim the seam to ⅛" (3 mm).

- Turn the dress right side out by pulling the facing through the space at each shoulder between the neck and armhole. Use a hemostat.

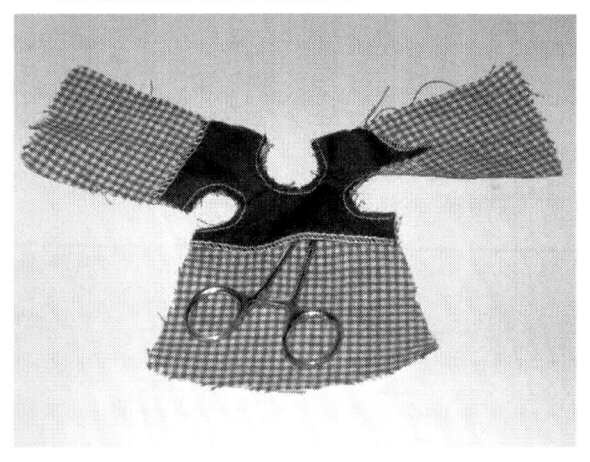

Grasp first back facing with hemostat.

Pull facing through first shoulder space.

Continue pulling first facing.

30

First facing pulled through.

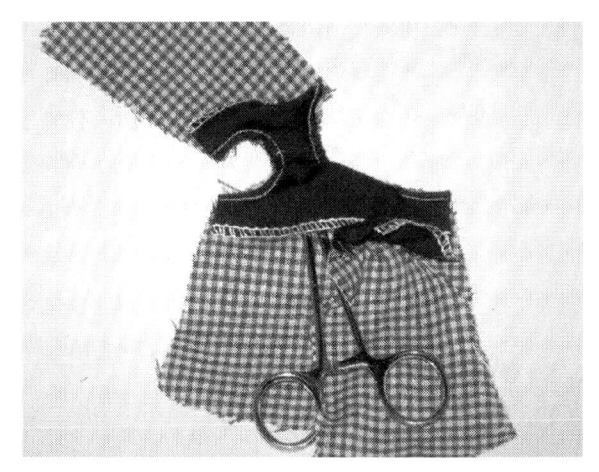

Grasp second back facing with hemostat.

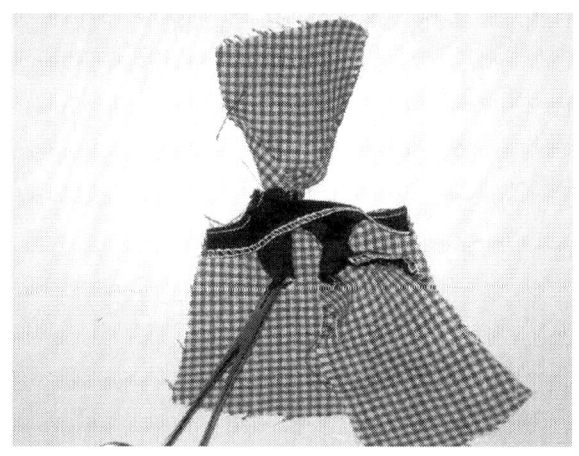

Pull second facing through.

Both facings pulled through.

- Press
- Topstitch around neck and armholes. (Optional)

Applying Optional Zipper

- If you plan to use a zipper follow these instructions. Otherwise go to the topic *Sewing Side Seams*. Applying a zipper may require more advanced skills than applying hook and loop tape. Putting in this tiny zipper is a good way to learn them. With a little practice you will be proud of your zipper skills.
- Finish the right facing opening and right back opening together as though they were one piece of fabric. Then finish the left back opening and left facing opening in the same manner. As you finish the edges zigzag or serge next to the raw edge, so that the total ½" (12 mm) seam allowance will be available.
- Measure 2½" (6 cm) down from the top of the back opening and mark with a pin or air soluble pen.
- Match the left and right back openings with right sides together. Start at the top of the opening. Sew a ½" (12 mm) seam with a machine basting stitch.
- Stop sewing at the 2½" (6 cm) mark.
- Cut the machine threads.
- Shorten the machine stitch length and continue sewing to the bottom of the dress.
- Press the seam open.

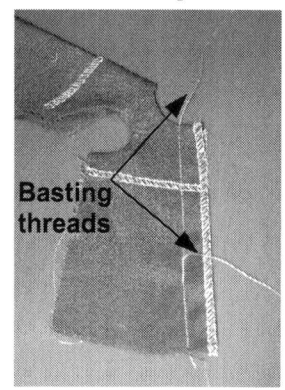

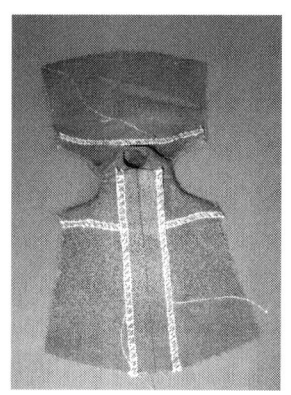

Basting threads

- Start with the zipper zipped up.

- Fold each side of the top edges of the zipper tape on the wrong side of the zipper until they meet the zipper pull. A little glue stick will hold the edges down.

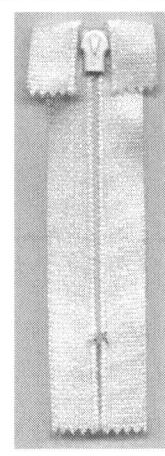

- Lay the zipper on the back closing. The right side of the zipper should be touching the dress back. The machine basting line should be between the zipper's teeth. The metal stop at the bottom of the zipper's teeth should be at the bottom of the basted section.
- Starting at the top of the zipper, hand baste the zipper to the back closing. Use the tape line that runs parallel to the teeth as a guide for a straight stitch.
- Place the zipper foot on the machine. Set the needle to the right of the zipper foot.
- Start at the top of the back opening and to the left of the zipper teeth. Sew on the wrong side of the dress back, and on top of the zipper tape.

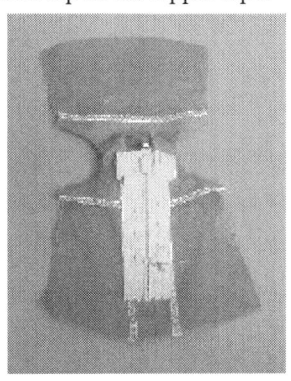

- Use the guide line on the zipper tape to sew a straight stitch. Sew down the tape. Sew just past the metal stop at the end of the teeth. Pivot the needle at the bottom of the stop.
- Sew across the center back seam to the second zipper guide line.
- Pivot the needle at the guide line and sew up the zipper tape to the top of the dress.

- Remove the basting thread.

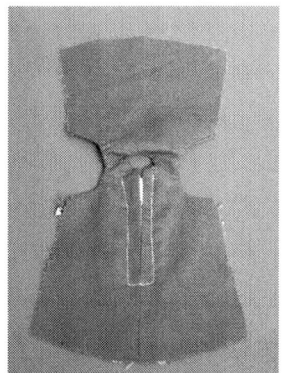

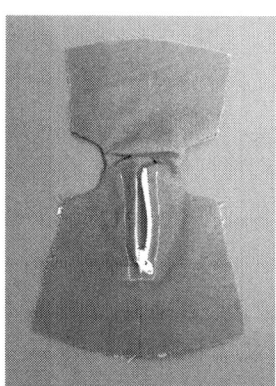

Sewing Side Seams

- Fold the dress at the shoulders right sides together. Match the double notches at the side seams.
- Sew side seams.
- Finish side seams.

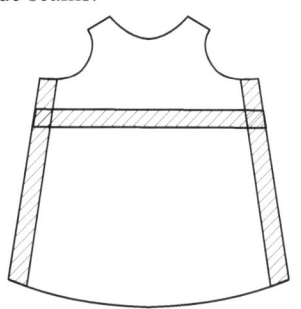

- Turn right side out.
- Press.

Back Openings

- If you did not apply a zipper, finish the right facing and right back together as though they were one piece of fabric. Then finish the left back opening and left facing in the same manner.
- Press each back opening ½" (12 mm) to the inside.
- Use **Tips** (p 69) for instructions on applying hook and loop tape.

Hem

- Finish the bottom edge of the dress.
- Run a gathering stitch around the finished bottom edge of the dress.
- Press a ½" (12 mm) hem in the dress.
- Pull the gathering stitch as you press, so that the hem lies flat inside the dress.
- Slip-stitch the hem.

Decorations

- If you like, add buttons or small appliques at the center front.

Short Jacket

Cutting and Marking

- Cut two fronts and two front linings.
- Cut one back and one back lining on fold.
- Mark the notches.

Lining the Jacket

- Match single notches at should/sleeve top for jacket.
- Sew jacket together at shoulder/sleeve top.

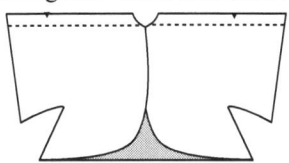

- Press seams open.
- Sew the same seams for lining.
- Press seams open.
- Right sides together pin or baste jacket to the lining.
- Sew jacket front and neck to lining and the bottom of jacket back to lining.

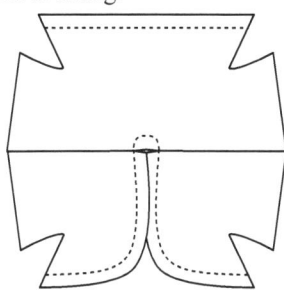

- Clip corners and curves.

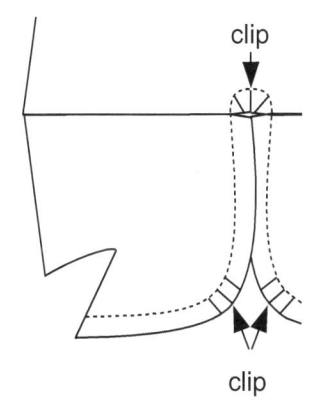

- Turn jacket right side out through unsewn sides and sleeves.

Jacket ready for turning.

Pull first side through sleeve opening.

Continue pulling first side through opening.

Finish turning jacket.

- Press.

Finishing the Jacket

- Finish the lining and sleeve edge together as if they were a single piece of fabric.

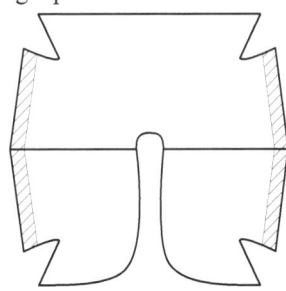

- Press the sleeve edge ¼" (6 mm) to the inside.
- Topstitch.
- Fold jacket right sides together at shoulder/sleeve top.

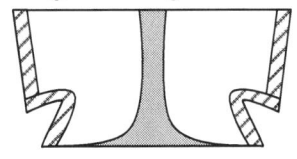

- Match double notches.
- Sew around sleeve bottoms and jacket sides.
- Finish seams. Zigzagging is the easiest method for finishing these small curves.
- Turn right side out
- Press.
- Topstitch around the outside of the jacket. (optional)

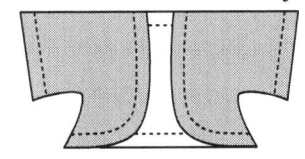

Bloomers

Cutting and Marking

- Cut two of the bloomers pattern.
- Mark the notches.

Making the Leg Casing and Inserting Elastic

- Finish the raw edges at the bottom of each leg.
- Press ½" (12 mm) to the inside at each leg bottom.
- Topstitch ¼ to ⅜" (6 to 9 mm) from the folded edge of each leg.

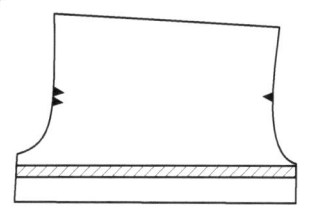

- Insert the elastic into the casing. Sew one end of the elastic along the raw edge of the casing.
- Gather the casing fabric over the elastic without stretching the elastic to about 2½" (6 cm).
- Try each bloomer half around the doll's leg and adjust the fit if necessary.
- Secure the second side of the elastic and cut off the excess.

Sewing the Center Front

- Match the single notches and sew the center fronts together.
- Finish the seam. Finish the two raw edges together, so that they can be pressed in one direction. If the seam is pressed open, it will be difficult to insert the elastic once the casing is constructed.

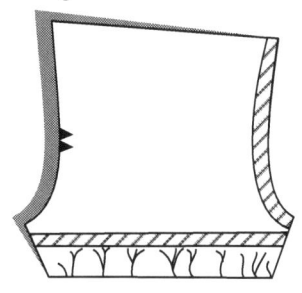

Making the Waist Casing and Inserting Elastic

- Finish the raw edge at the top of the waist. Press the fabric in ½" (12 mm) to the inside.
- Topstitch ¼" to ⅜" (6 to 9 mm) from the folded edge at the top of the bloomers.

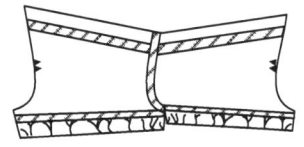

- Insert the elastic into the casing. Sew one end of the elastic along the raw edge of the casing
- Gather the casing fabric to 4½" (11 cm) over the elastic without stretching the elastic.
- Try the bloomers around the doll's waist and adjust if necessary. Secure the second side of the elastic and cut off the excess.

Finishing the Pants

- Sew center backs together. Finish the seam.

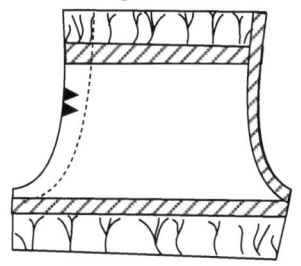

- Bring the center fronts and center backs together and sew the inside leg seams.

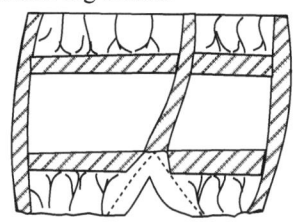

- Turn right side out.

A-line Dress with Short Jacket and Bloomer

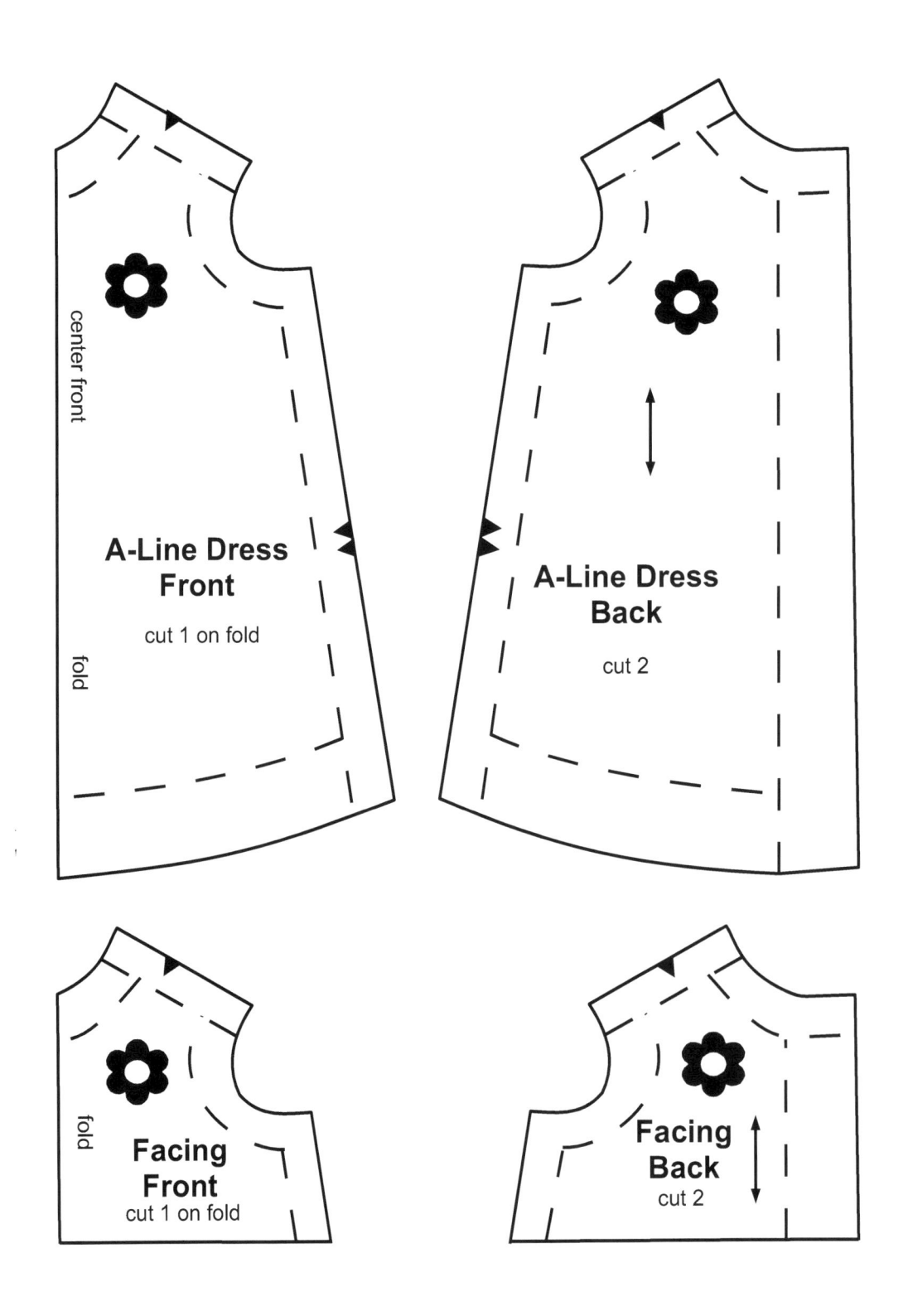

A-Line Dress Front
cut 1 on fold

center front
fold

A-Line Dress Back
cut 2

Facing Front
cut 1 on fold

fold

Facing Back
cut 2

A-line Dress with Short Jacket and Bloomer

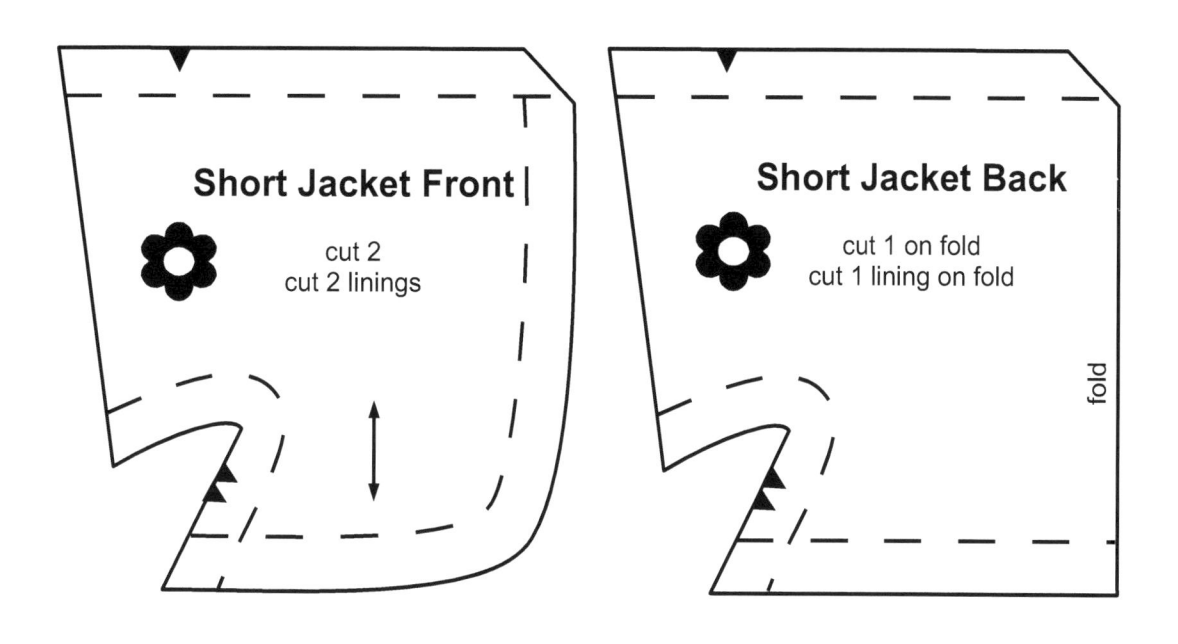

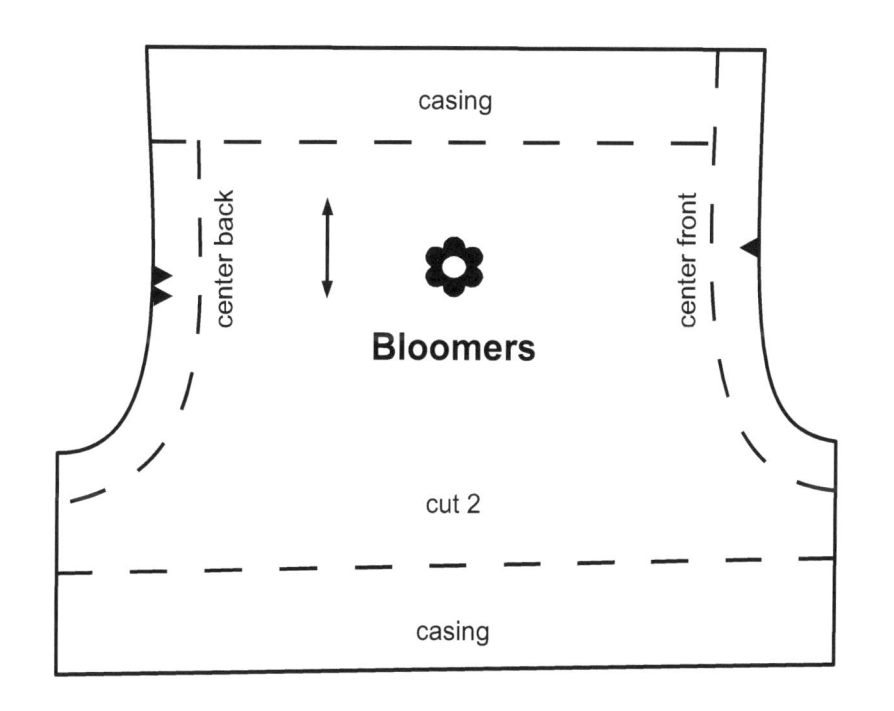

Sewing a Small Doll and Her Clothing
www.sherralynsdolls.com

Pants, T-Shirt, and Skirt

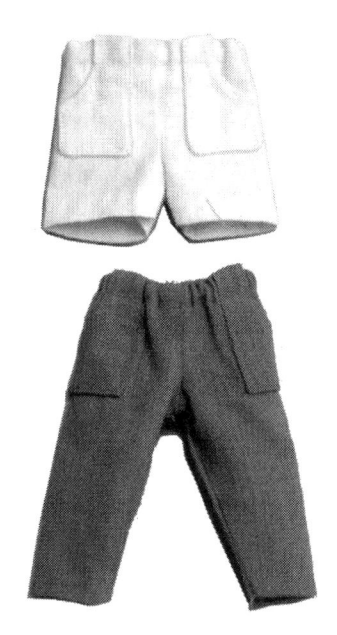

Supplies

- Cotton broadcloth in the color or design of your choice for Pants, Shorts, and Skirt
- Optional blue or khakis colored broadcloth for jeans or khakis
- T-shirt knit in color of your choice
- Matching or contrasting ribbing (sometimes T-shirt knit works as a ribbing substitute)
- Matching thread
- Optional orange thread for jeans topstitching
- Sewing glue stick for optional pockets

Equipment

- Basic sewing tools (see **Tools, Tips, and Techniques**)
- Optional hemostat to turn pocket for pants and skirt

Skills

- Pants and skirt without pockets (easy projects)
  - Use **Tools, Tips, and Techniques** for any help that you need
- Optional applying a patch pocket to pants and skirt to make jeans and khakis (advanced project explained in the instructions).
- T-shirt (more challenging project than simple pants and skirt)
  - Attaching a neck band (explained in the instructions)
  - Sewing knit with a zigzag stitch (explained in the instructions)
  - Setting in a sleeve (explained in the instructions)
  - Applying hook and loop tape (**Tools, Tips, and Techniques**)

Sizes

- Florabunda's (✿) Clothing Patterns Fit
  - Sherralyn's Dolls' Florabunda
  - Madam Alexander's® 7½" (19 cm) Wendy
  - Vogue Doll Company's® Modern and Vintage Ginny®
  - Lillian Vernon's® 7½" (19 cm) doll

Introduction

These instructions describe the construction of long pants, shorts, A-line skirt, optional pockets, and T-shirt for Florabunda and other 7½" to 8" (19 to 20 cm) dolls.

Symbols

- The pattern pieces for Florabunda's clothing patterns are marked by a flower (✿)
- In these instructions light gray indicates the right side of the fabric

Pants

Cutting and Marking

- Cut two of the jeans or shorts pattern.
- Mark the notches.

Applying Patch Pockets (optional)

- If you do not wish to apply pockets, go to the section marked *Finishing the Pants Leg Bottoms*.
- This method of applying pockets makes it easier to produce pockets of a consistent size and shape.
- Fold a small scrap of pants fabric in half right sides together.
- Draw two pockets on the folded fabric by tracing around the pocket template.
- Sew on the traced lines.
- Leave the top of the pocket open.
- Cut out pockets using a ⅛" (3 mm) seam allowance. Note the clipped corners.

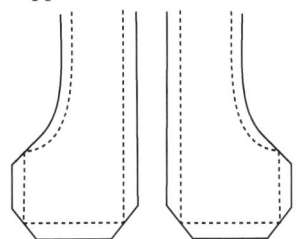

- Turn pockets right side out and press.
- Topstitch the curved area that will be left open when the pocket is sewn to the pants. Use gold or orange thread for the blue jeans if you like.

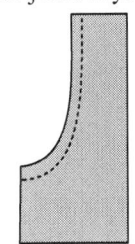

- Mark the pocket placement on the right side of the pants fabric with air soluble pen.
- Place pockets over placement markings.
- Pin in place or use sewing glue stick.
- Topstitch around the three straight areas of the pocket. Leave the previously stitched curved area open. Use orange or gold thread for blue jeans if you like.

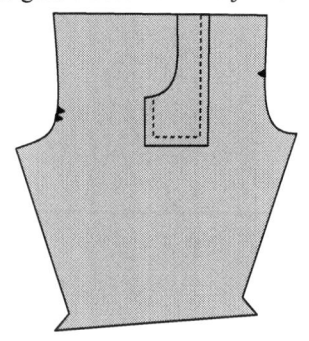

Finishing the Pants Leg Bottoms

- Finish the raw edges at the bottom of each leg.
- Turn ¼" (6 mm) to the inside at each leg bottom.
- Topstitch and press.

Making the Casing and Inserting Elastic

- Match the single notches and sew the center fronts together.
- Finish the seam. Finish the two raw edges together, so that they can be pressed in one direction. If the seam is pressed open, it will be difficult to insert the elastic once the casing is constructed.

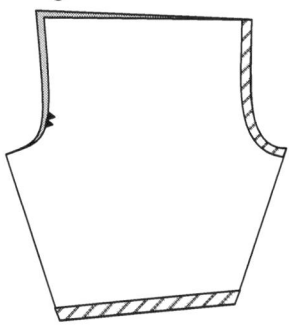

- Finish the raw edge at the top of the waist. Press the fabric in ½" (12 mm) to the inside.
- Topstitch ¼" to ⅜" (6 to 9 mm) from the folded edge at the top of the pants.
- Insert the elastic into the casing. Sew one end of the elastic along the raw edge of the casing.
- Gather the casing fabric to 4½" (11 cm) over the elastic without stretching the elastic.

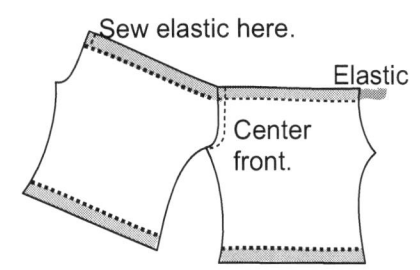

- Try the pants around the doll's waist and adjust if necessary. Secure the second side of the elastic by sewing across it through the casing several times. Cut off the excess elastic.

Finishing the Pants

- Match the double notches and sew center backs together. 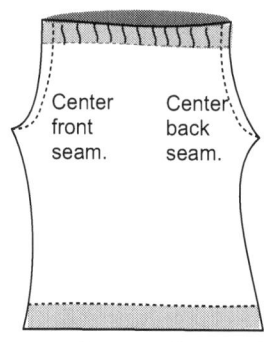
- Bring the center fronts and center backs together and sew the inside leg seams. 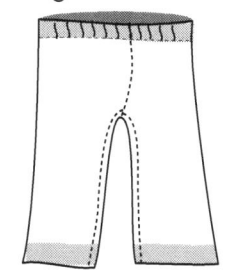
- Turn right side out.

Skirt

Cutting and Marking

- Cut one front and one back skirt from the skirt pattern.
- Mark the notches.

Applying Patch Pockets

- If you do not wish to apply pockets, go to the section marked *Making the Casing and Inserting Elastic*.
- This method of applying pockets makes it easier to produce pockets of a consistent size and shape.
- Fold a small scrap of skirt fabric in half right sides together.
- Draw two skirt pockets on the folded fabric by tracing around the skirt pocket template.
- Sew on the traced lines.
- Leave the top and sides of the pocket open.
- Cut out pockets using a ⅛" (3 mm) seam allowance. 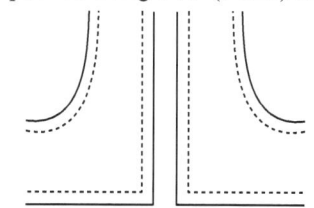
- Turn pockets right side out.
- Topstitch the curved area that will be left open when the pocket is sewn to the skirt. Use gold or orange thread for a blue jean skirt if you like. 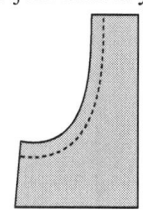
- Mark the pocket placement on the right side of the skirt fabric with air soluble pen. Mark the pockets on only one cut skirt piece. The pockets will define the skirt front.
- Place pockets over placement markings.
- Pin in place or use sewing glue stick.
- Topstitch around the two straight areas that will not be caught in the seam. Use orange or gold thread for a blue jean skirt, if you like.

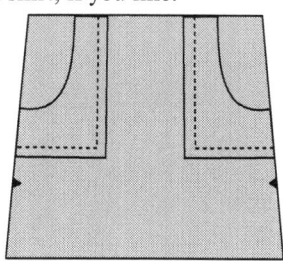

Making the Casing and Inserting Elastic

- Sew one side of the skirt front to the skirt back matching the single notches.
- Finish the seam. Finish the two raw edges together, so that they can be pressed in one direction. If the seam is pressed open, it will be difficult to insert the elastic once the casing is constructed.
- To make the casing open the skirt up and finish the raw edge at the top of the waist.
- Press the fabric in ½" (12 mm) to the inside.
- Top stitch ¼" to ⅜" (6 to 9 mm) from the folded edge at the top of the skirt.
- Insert the elastic into the casing. Sew one end of the elastic along a raw edge of the casing opening. 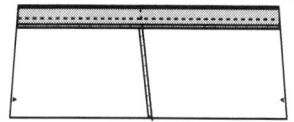
- Gather the casing fabric to 4½" (11 cm) over the elastic without stretching the elastic.
- Try the skirt around the doll's waist and adjust if necessary. Secure the second side of the elastic and cut off the excess.

Finishing the skirt

- Finish the raw edge at the bottom of the skirt.
- If you would like to topstitch the hem, press the hem ½" (12 mm) to the inside and topstitch.
- Sew the second side of skirt front to skirt back, matching single notches.

- Finish the seam.
- If you plan to slip-stitch the hem, sew the second side of skirt front to skirt back before hemming.
- Press the hem ½" (12 mm) to the inside and slip-stitch.
- Turn right side out.

T-shirt

Cutting and Marking

- Cut one front on fold, two backs, two sleeves, and one neck ribbing. The neck ribbing should be cut from real ribbing, if you have it. Sometimes, when the knit is stretchy enough, T-shirt knit works as a ribbing substitute.
- Check arrows before cutting to make certain the patterns are aligned correctly with the fabric's stretch.
- Mark circle on the sleeves.

Sewing Knit with Zigzag Seams

- Use zigzag stitches to join T-shirt. I have not had success using a serger on these small T-shirts.
- Use a fairly wide zigzag stitch to join knits. Set the zigzags to be fairly close together, but not a satin stitch.
- Note that the seam allowance is only ⅛" (3 mm).
- If your zigzag is less than ⅛" (3 mm) wide, you may trim the seam.

Sewing the Shoulder Seams

- Right sides together match single notches at shoulder seams.
- Sew shoulder seams.

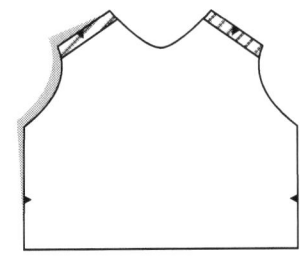

Attaching the Neckband

- Fold the ribbing in half with wrong sides together.
- Press.
- Place the folded ribbing on the right side of the shirt with the raw edges next to the neck raw edge.
- Do not fold the back closing to the inside until the ribbing has been sown to the neck. Start applying ribbing at the raw edge of the shirt back.
- Stretch the ribbing with gentle consistent pressure while zigzagging it to the neck. The ribbing must be stretched to fit the neck.

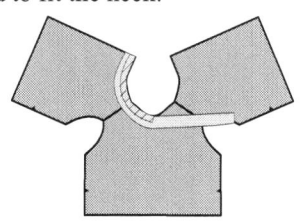

Setting in Sleeves

- Press the sleeve hem ¼" (6 mm) to the inside of the fabric and zigzag.
- Match the dot at the top of the sleeve to the shoulder seam.
- Right sides together, pin and then hand baste the sleeve into the arm opening. 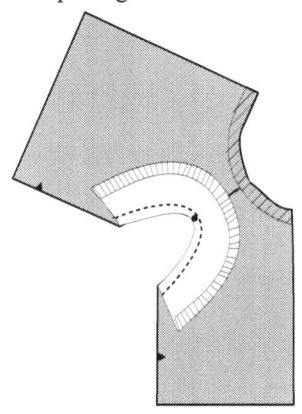
- Zigzag the sleeve to the shirt.

Finishing the T-shirt

- Match the single notches on the shirt sides and zigzag across the sleeves and down the sides.
- Press the T-shirt hem and zigzag. 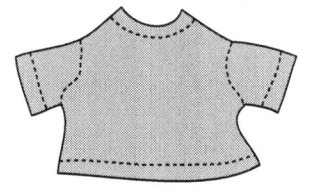
- Press both back openings ½" (12 mm) under.
- Apply hook and loop tape to back openings.
- Turn under the raw edge at the bottom of the T-shirt ½" (12 cm) and zigzag the hem.

Pants, T-Shirt, and Skirt

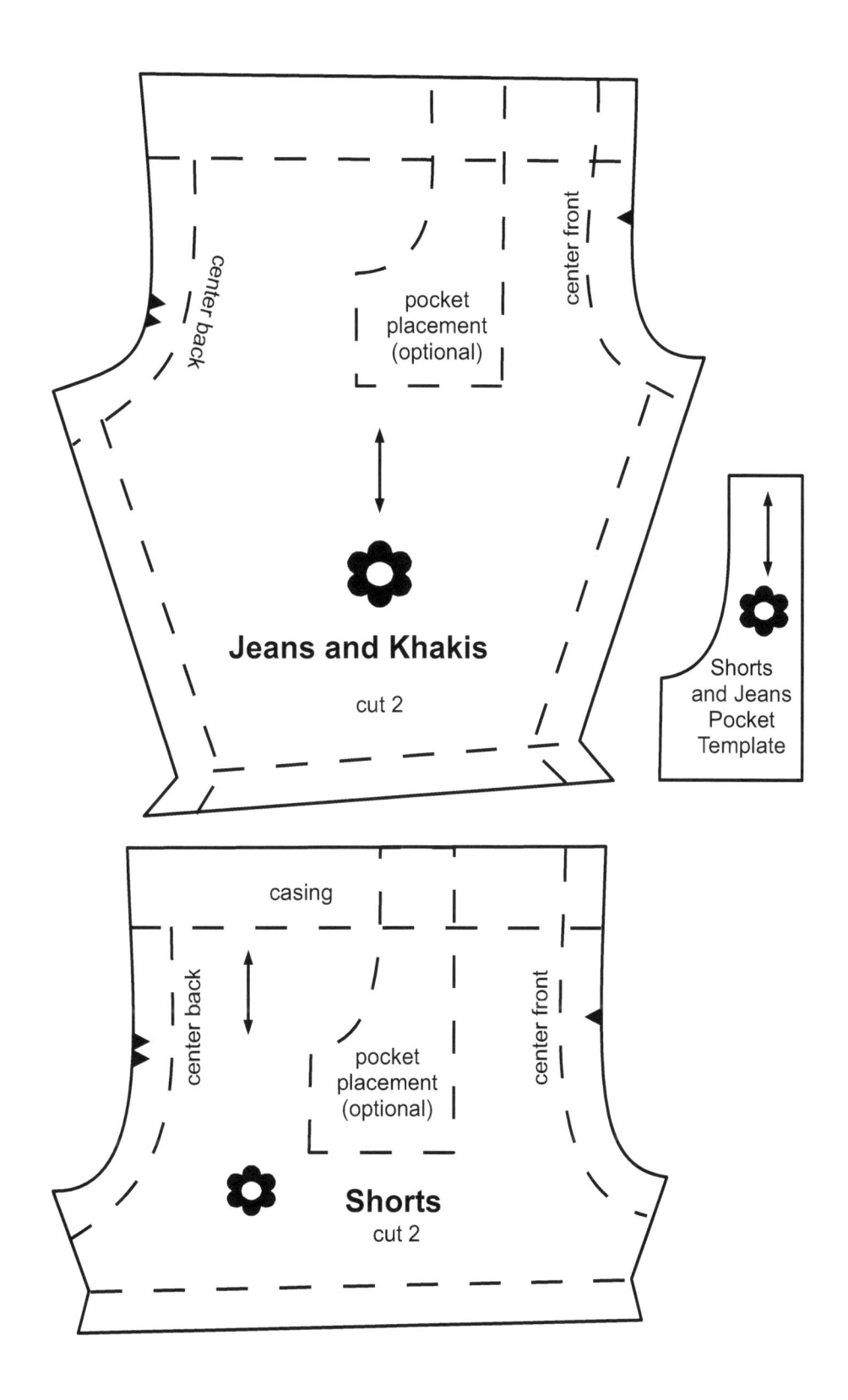

Jeans and Khakis

cut 2

center back

center front

pocket placement (optional)

Shorts and Jeans Pocket Template

Shorts

cut 2

casing

center back

center front

pocket placement (optional)

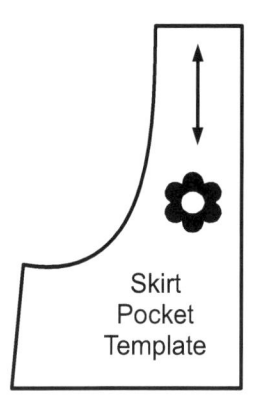

Pants, T-Shirt, and Skirt

Skirt Pocket Template

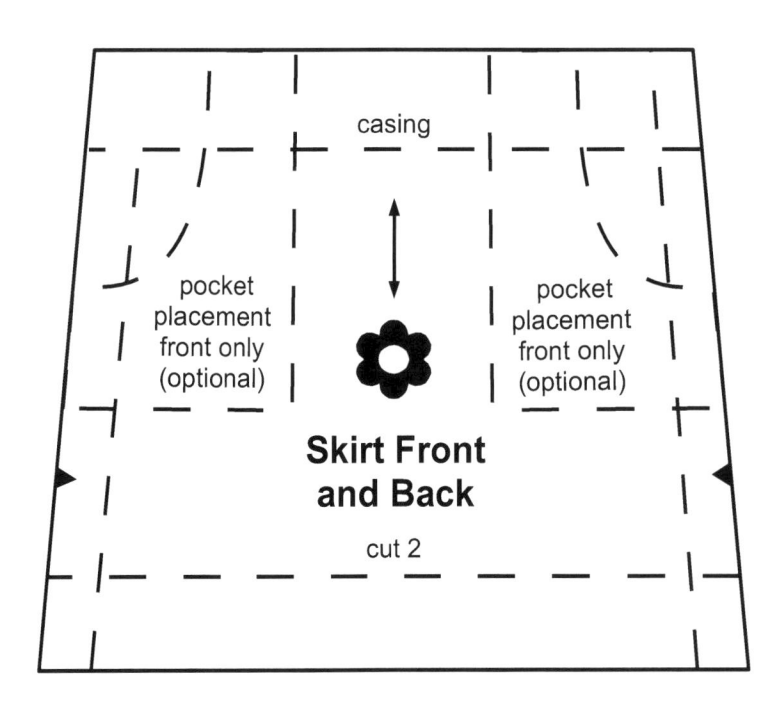

casing

pocket placement front only (optional)

pocket placement front only (optional)

Skirt Front and Back

cut 2

Pants, T-Shirt, and Skirt

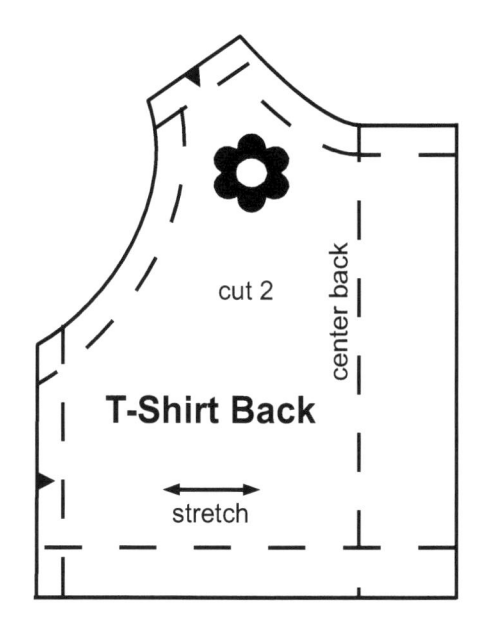

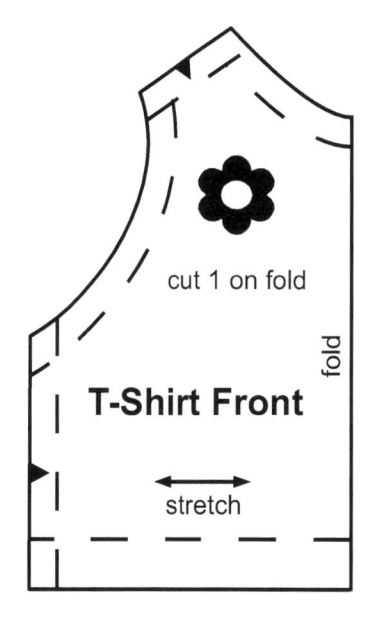

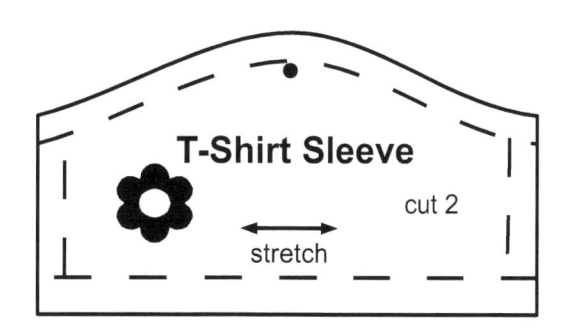

45

Sewing a Small Doll and Her Clothing
www.sherralynsdolls.com

Ballgown and Classic Dress

Supplies

- Scraps of silky or cotton fabric
- Matching thread
- ½" to ¾" (12 to 19 mm) lace edging (Gold or sliver metallic lace adds a nice touch to the ball gown.)
- Plain or metallic rickrack (optional)
- Embroidery floss or metallic pearl for sewing rickrack (optional) - Metallic pearl is a type of embroidery floss found in the embroidery section of craft stores. It is also used for making the Crown.
- 5" (13 cm) of ⅝" (15 mm) ribbon for ribbon flower (optional)
- Small bead for ribbon flower center (optional)
- Optional gold or silver trim for crown
- Optional craft store gems for crown

Equipment

- Basic sewing tools (see **Tools, Tips, and Techniques**)
- Crewel needles for applying optional rickrack and sewing the crown

Skills

- Applying gathered lace to neck opening
- Applying ungathered lace to hem
- Attaching a cuff to a sleeve
- Applying rickrack (optional)
- Making a ribbon flower (optional)
- Setting in a sleeve
- Joining a gathered skirt to a dress bodice
- Applying hook and loop tape (Use **Tools, Tips, and Techniques**)
- Making a crown using metallic trim

Sizes

- Florabunda's (✿) Clothing Patterns Fit
  - Sherralyn's Dolls' Florabunda
  - Madam Alexander's® 7½" (19 cm) Wendy
  - Vogue Doll Company's® Modern and Vintage Ginny®
  - Lillian Vernon's® 7½" (19 cm) doll

Introduction

These instructions describe the construction of a ballgown, classic dress and a princess crown for Florabunda and other 7½" to 8" (19 to 20 cm) dolls.

Symbols

- The pattern pieces for Florabunda's clothing patterns are marked by a flower (✿)
- In the patterns a thick broken line indicates where to gather the fabric.

  ||||||||||||||

- In these instructions light gray indicates the right side of the fabric

Ballgown and Classic Dress

The ballgown and dress are made using the same steps. The ballgown is made with silkier fabric. It uses the longer skirt pattern. The ballgown can also be made with metallic laces and trims to give it the "royal" look.

Cutting and Marking

- Cut one front on the fold and two backs.
- Cut two sleeves and two sleeve cuffs.
- Choose either the long or short version of the skirt and cut one skirt on the fold.
- Mark the notches.
- Mark the dot at the top of each sleeve.
- The fold lines of the skirt and bodice front indicate the center front of the dress. Mark the center front on both pieces using a pin or air soluble pen.

Sewing Shoulder/Sleeve Seams

- Match the single notches at the shoulder.
- Sew shoulder seams and finish the seams.
- Press the finished seam to the back of the garment.

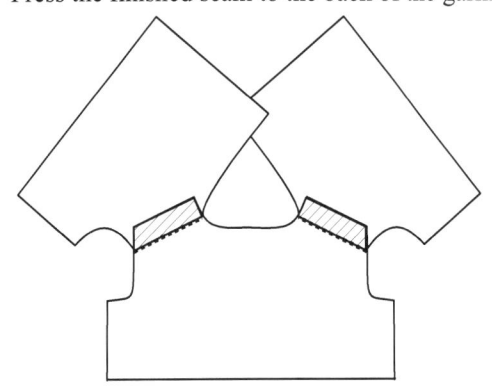

Attaching Lace to the Neck

- Cut a strip of lace about 8" (20 cm) long.
- Pull a thread in the heading of the lace until it fits the neckline of the bodice. If the chosen lace does not have a heading thread, sew a gathering thread by hand or machine and pull the thread until the lace fits the neckline.

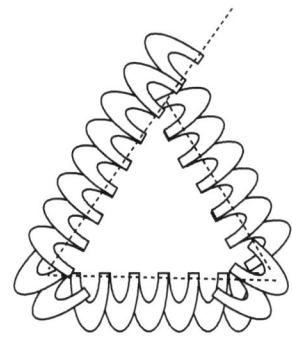

- Lay the right side of the lace on the wrong side of the fabric. The heading edge of the lace should be next to the raw edge of the fabric at the neckline.
- Adjust the machine setting to a short zigzag. The zigzag threads should be close enough together that they almost make a satin stitch. The zigzag should be the width of the lace heading.
- Zigzag the lace and fabric together.

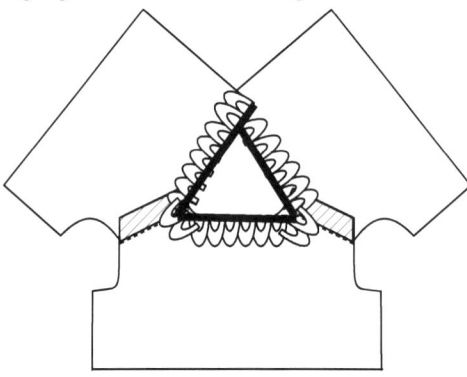

- Turn the lace to the right side of the fabric.
- Zigzag over the original zigzag seam.

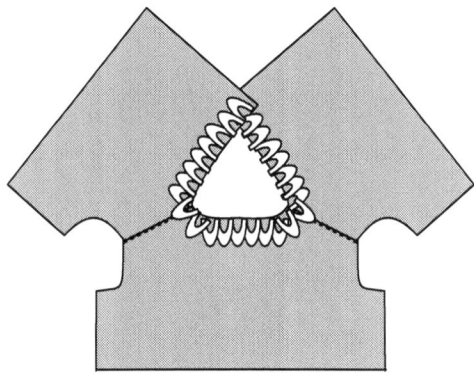

Sewing a Cuff on Sleeves

- Before sewing the cuff to the sleeve, check the fit on your doll.
  - Pin the two short sides together.
  - Try to pull the doll's hand through the cuff.
  - If the hand does not go through the cuff, cut a slightly longer cuff.
- Finish one side of the cuff.

- Sew two rows of gathering stitches at the bottom of each sleeve.

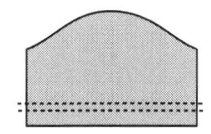

- Pull up the bottom of sleeve to fit the cuff.

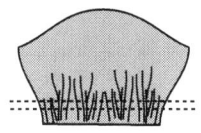

- Right sides together sew the unfinished side of the cuff to the bottom of the sleeve.

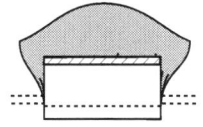

- Remove the gathering stitches.
- Fold the cuff to the inside of the sleeve as indicated on the pattern.
- Stitch the folded cuff to the sleeve.

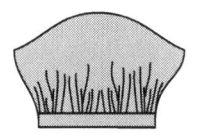

Sewing Rickrack to Cuff and Waist (optional)

- Use metallic rickrack and matching metallic pearl for the ballgown if you wish.
- Use matching or contrasting embroidery floss to sew plain rickrack to the classic dress.
- Bring the needle to the outside of the sleeve cuff or waist line under the first rickrack peak. Pull all of the thread through the fabric.
- Insert the needle into the fabric over a rickrack valley. Pull all the thread to the back of the fabric.
- The thread should lay across the rickrack.
- Bring the needle to the outside of the fabric under the next rickrack peak.
- Continue crossing the thread over the rickrack in the same manner.

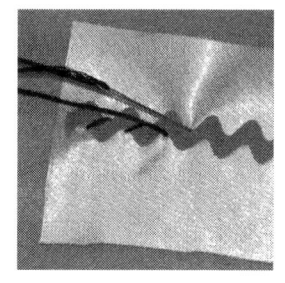

- Never pierce the rickrack with the needle.
- Pull the thread all the way through the fabric each time the needle goes through the fabric.
- Secure the thread on the wrong side of the fabric.

Setting in the Sleeves

- Hand gather the top of each sleeve where indicated on the pattern.

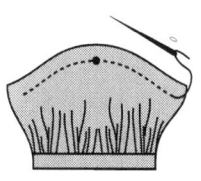

- Pull up the gathers to fit the arm hole of the bodice. Secure the gathering thread.
- Right sides together pin and then hand baste each sleeve to the bodice. Match the dot at the top of the sleeve to the shoulder seams.
- Machine stitch each sleeve to the bodice.

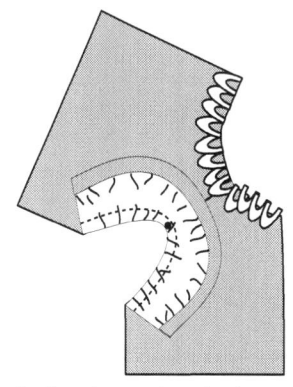

- Remove the basting and gathering stitches.
- Finish the seam with a zigzag stitch. A serger does not work well on such a small curve.

Sewing Bodice sides

- Fold right sides of bodice together at the shoulder seams.
- Sew across the bottom of each sleeve and down the bodice's side.

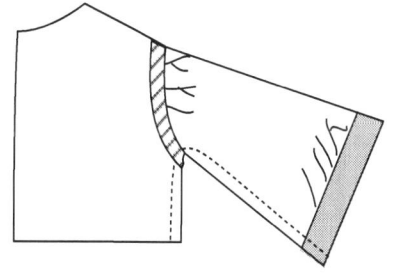

- Finish the seams.

Preparing the Skirt

- Lay the right side of the lace chosen for the hem on the right side of the fabric. Do not gather the lace.
- The heading edge of the lace should be next to the raw edge of the skirt bottom.
- Adjust the machine setting to a short zigzag. The zigzag threads should be close enough together that they almost make a satin stitch. The zigzag should be the width of the lace heading.

49

- Zigzag the lace and fabric together.

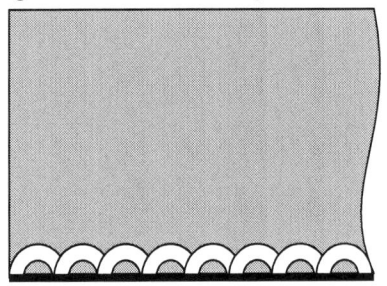

- Pull the lace down below the fabric and press.
- The zigzagged seam will be on the inside of the skirt hem.

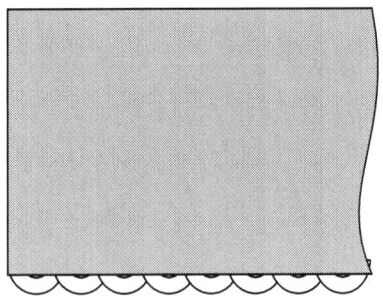

- Topstitch on the fabric very close to the lace using a straight stitch.

Gathering the Skirt

- Sew two rows of gathering stitches across the top of the skirt as indicated on the pattern.

- Pull up the gathering stitches to fit the bottom of the bodice

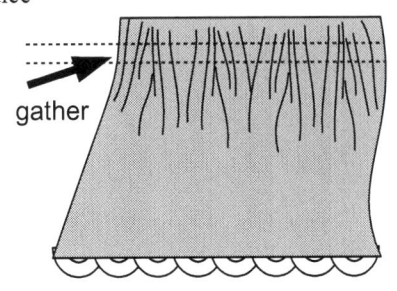

.Attaching the Skirt to the Bodice

- Match the center fronts and pin the skirt to the bodice. You may baste them together if you like.
- Sew the skirt to the bodice.
- Remove the gathering stitches and optional basting stitches.
- Finish the seam.

Adding Rickrack and Ribbon Flower (Optional)

- To sew rickrack at waist seam, follow instructions above titled: *Sewing Rickrack to Cuff and Waist*.
- To make the optional flower:
  - Apply seam sealant on each end of a 5" (13 cm) piece of ribbon.
  - Turn under ⅛" (3 mm) of ribbon at one end of the ribbon.
  - Begin at the end you have turned under, take small gathering stitches down the length of the ribbon.

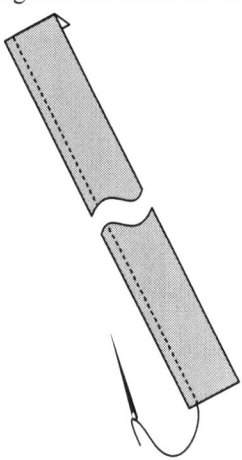

  - Pull the gathers to make a circle with the ribbon.

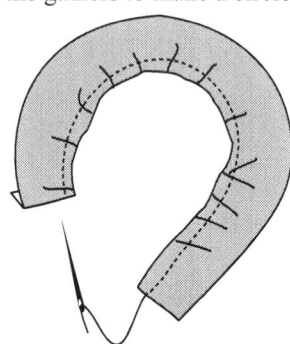

  - Overlap ⅛" to ¼" (3 to 6 mm) of ribbon at the end of the gathered circle.

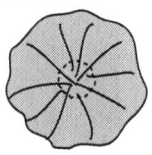

  - Sew a small bead in the middle of the circle.

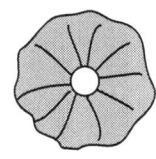

- If you enjoy experimenting, you might try making a flower with rickrack.

Closing the Back

- Finish the back seams.
- Press each back opening ½" (12 mm) to the inside.

- Use **Tips** (p 69) for instructions on applying hook and loop tape.

Princess Crown

This Crown is an easy and enjoyable project. To make it, you need to sew a few hand stitches and glue on the royal jewels.

- Measure around the doll's head where she will wear the crown.

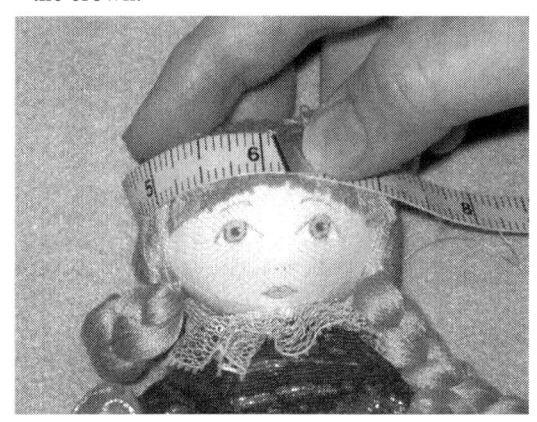

- Cut a length of trim ¼" (6 mm) longer than the measurement.

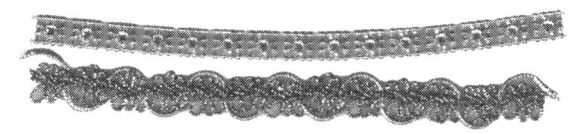

- Cut an optional higher front for the crown. The length should be ¼" (6 mm) longer than the finished length of the front piece.
- Add seam sealant to the ends.

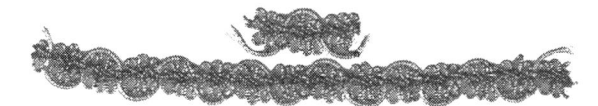

- If you have cut a higher front piece, turn under the seam allowances and sew it to the middle of the crown.

- Glue on the jewels.

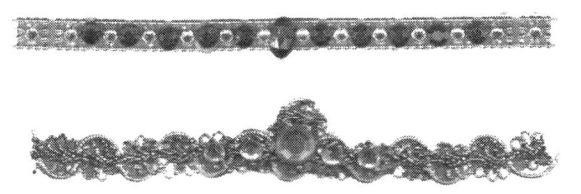

- Turn under a ⅛" (3 mm) seam allowance, and sew the ends together to make a circle.

Ballgown and Classic Dress

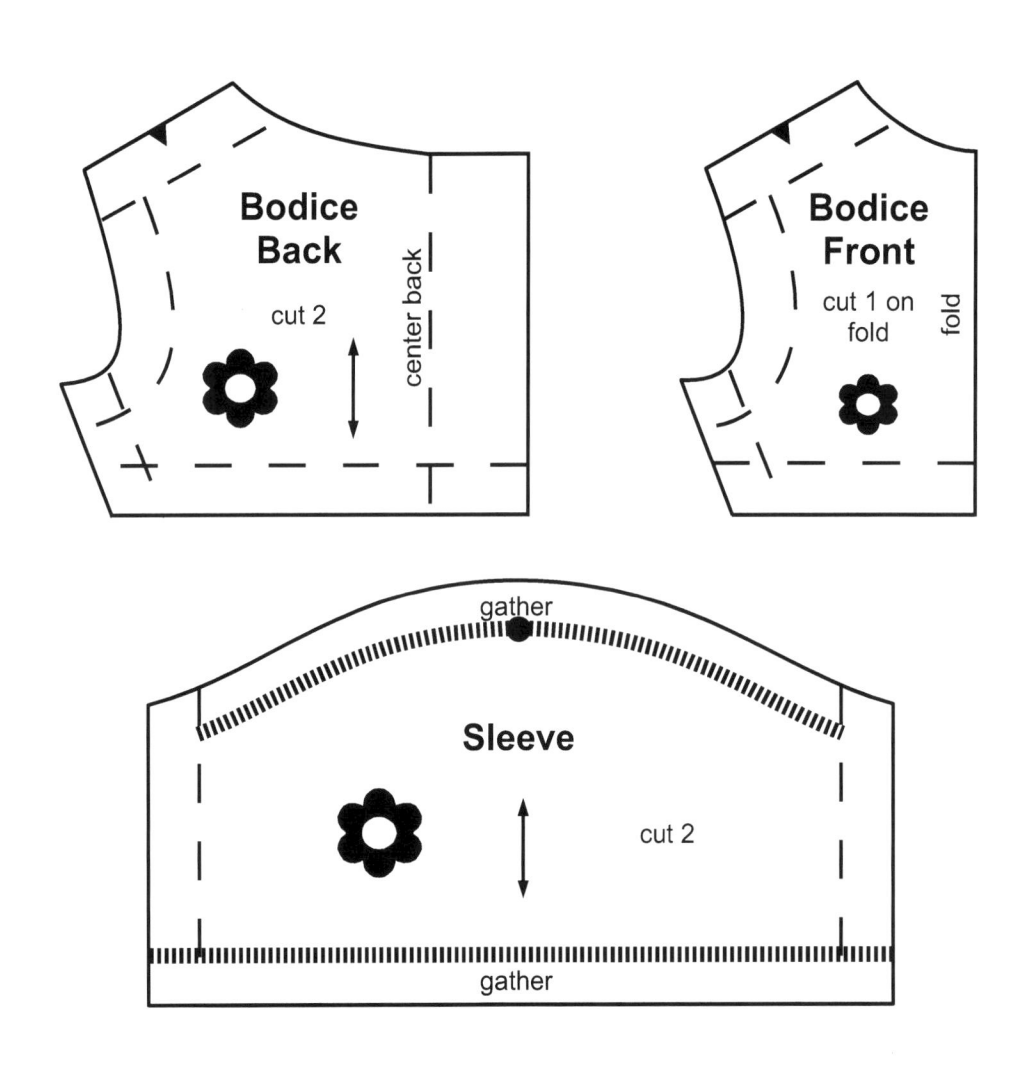

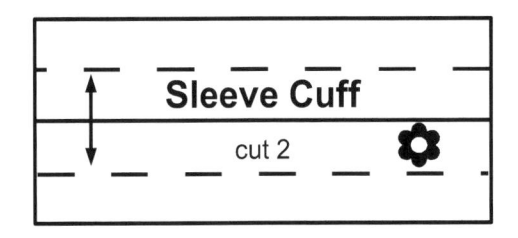

52

Ballgown and Classic Dress

center back

gather

Skirt

Cut here for short skirt

Cut here for long skirt

fold

Short skirt 2¾" x 9¼" (7 cm x 23 cm)
Long skirt 4" x 9¼" (10 cm x 23 cm)

Sewing a Small Doll and Her Clothing
www.sherralynsdolls.com

Shoes and Socks

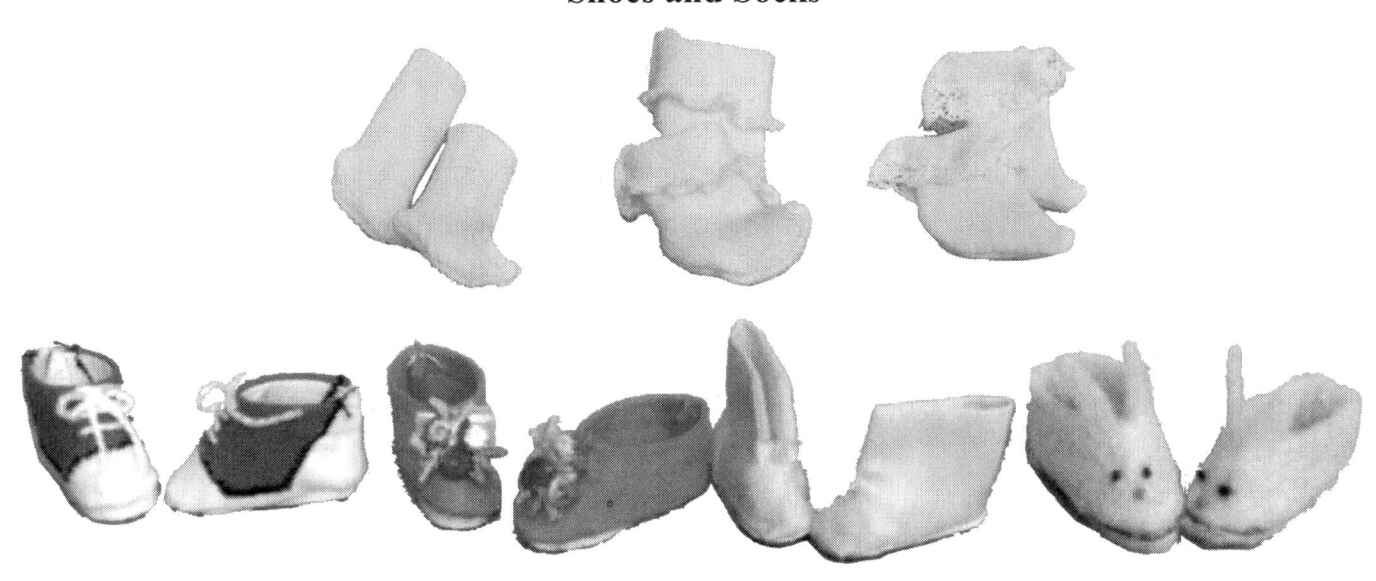

Supplies

- Woven fabric in the color of your choice for shoe last, shoe, sneaker overlay, boot, and linings
- White fabric for sneaker and lining
- Pink or white felt for bunny slipper
- Sewable fusible webbing for linings and sneaker overlay
- Seam sealant
- Felt for sole (I like stiff felt)
- Index card for insole
- Tacky glue
- Optional buttons, bows, or small appliques for shoes
- Pearl cotton for laces for sneakers
- Black embroidery floss for the bunny slipper eyes
- Pink embroidery floss for bunny slipper nose
- Two pink or white ¼ " (6 mm) pompoms for bunny slipper tails
- Knit for socks (Use a thin sock or a stretchy knit fabric.)
- Optional narrow lace for top trim for socks
- Bamboo cooking skewer for shoe last
- Small amount of polyester stuffing for shoe last

Equipment

- Basic sewing tools (see **Tools, Tips, and Techniques**)
- Miniature clothes pins
- Size 20 or 22 tapestry needle

Skills

- Constructing a shoe by gluing sole and insole
- Applying lace to the top of a sock
- French knot for bunny eyes (Use **Tools, Tips, and Techniques.**)
- Constructing a shoe last to help in shoe making

Sizes

- Florabunda's (✿) Clothing Patterns Fit
  - Sherralyn's Dolls' Florabunda
  - Madam Alexander's® 7½" (19 cm) Wendy
  - Vogue Doll Company's® Modern and Vintage Ginny®
  - Lillian Vernon's® 7½" (19 cm) doll

Introduction

These instructions describe the construction of dress shoes, sneakers, bunny slippers, and boots for for Florabunda and other small dolls.

Symbols

- The pattern pieces for Florabunda's shoes are marked by a flower (✿).
- In the patterns and these instructions the location of clips is indicated by a small scissor icon and a gray line. 
- In the patterns a thick broken line indicates where to gather the fabric.
- In these instructions light gray indicates the right side of the fabric

Shoe Last

A last is a foot shaped object used in making a shoe. If you prefer not to use your doll's foot to help glue the shoes to their soles, you can make your own shoe last. Make the shoe last before beginning shoe construction. I made a "Shoe Last on a Stick" because I wanted a better way to hold the shoes and their soles together while I was gluing them. The shoe lasts are easy to make. If you like whimsy, they have a humorous or at least strange appearance.

- Trace around the shoe last template.
- Sew on folded fabric on the traced line. Leave the top of the shoe last and the toe area open.
- Cut out shoe last leaving a ⅛" (3 mm) seam. Leave a ¼" (6 mm) opening at the top and bottom of the foot. The larger seam allowance makes it easier to match the foot seams.

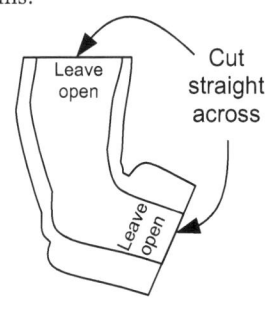

- Finger press the seams of toe open. Bring the top and bottom of the toe seams together. Match the seams carefully.
- Sew across the toe using a ¼" (6 mm) seam. 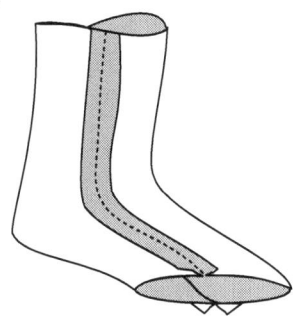
- Turn right side out and stuff. 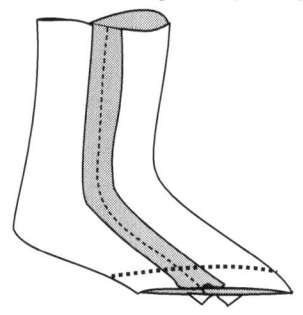
- Cut tip off skewer and poke into the middle of the shoe last. 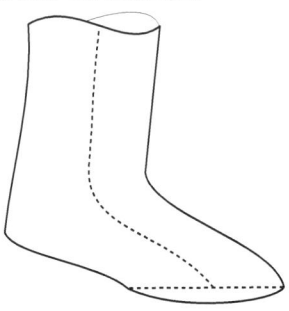
- Fold raw edges of the shoe last inside ¼" (6 mm).
- Gather the top of the shoe last around the skewer. 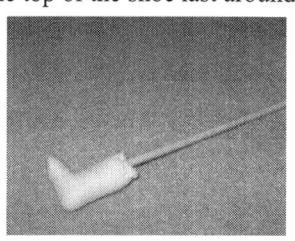
- To use the shoe last balance the flat edge of the stick on the seat of a chair. Hold the stick between your legs. The shoe last will be above your lap. Use it to support the shoe and insole while you glue insole to the shoe.
- Then use the shoe last to support the shoe and insole while you glue on the sole.

If you have some type of clamp and would prefer to work at table level, you can experiment with clamping the shoe last to hold it steady.

Dress Shoe

Cutting and Marking

- Cut out two shoes and two shoe linings.
- Cut out two soles from stiff felt.
- Cut out two insoles from an index card.

Sewing Shoes

- Back the lining fabric with fusible webbing meant for sewing.
- With right sides together sew shoe to shoe lining all the way across the top of the shoe. Use a ⅛" (3 mm) seam. The webbing side of the lining should be on the outside and not be touching the shoe fabric.
- Clip curve at the three places indicated on the seam that you have just sewn.

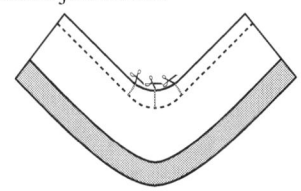

- Remove backing from the fusible webbing.
- Turn the shoe right side out so that the raw edges of the seam that you have just sewn are hidden. The webbing side of the lining should now be touching the shoe fabric.
- Press to fuse the lining to the shoe. Notice that the lining does not completely cover the shoe fabric. The remaining shoe fabric will be turned under and glued to the sole and insole.

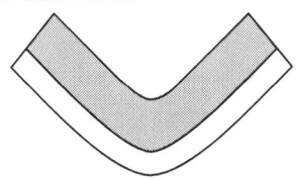

- Topstitch around the top of the shoe (optional)

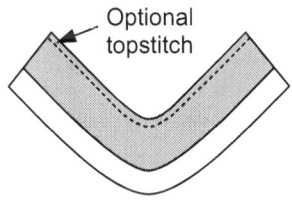

Optional topstitch

- Put seam sealant around the bottom of the shoe and let dry. (optional)
- Right sides together, bring the two short sides of the shoe together. Sew the ⅛" (3 mm) seam to make the shoe heel.
- Turn the shoe right side out.

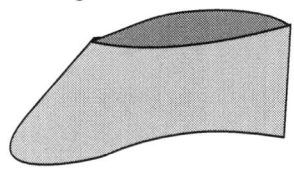

- Go to the section titled **Gluing the Sole and Insole.**

Bunny Slippers

Cutting and Marking

- Cut two bunny slippers from felt.
- Cut out two soles from stiff felt.
- Cut out two insoles from an index card.

Making Bunny Features

- Mark the eyes and nose on the right side of the felt with air soluble pen.
- Make a French knot for each eye using two strands of floss.
- Use three or five stitches with two strands of pink floss to make a triangular.

Sewing Slipper

- Stay stitch the bottom of the slipper ¼" (6 mm) from the raw edge. The fabric below the stay-stitch line will be turned under and glued to the sole and insole.

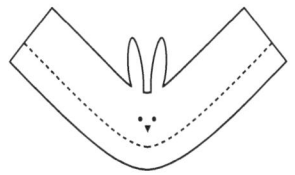

- Right sides together, bring the two short sides of the slipper together. Sew the ⅛" (3 mm) seam to make the slipper heel.
- Turn the slipper right side out.

- Go to the section titled **Gluing the Sole and Insole.**

Sneakers

Cutting and Marking

- Cut out two sneakers and two sneaker linings from white cotton fabric and two overlays from fabric color of your choice.
- Cut out two soles from stiff felt.
- Cut out two insoles from an index card.

Sewing the Sneaker.

- Back lining fabric and overlay fabric with fusible webbing.
- Fuse the sneaker overlay to the right side of the sneaker.

- Mark the eyelet holes with air soluble pen.

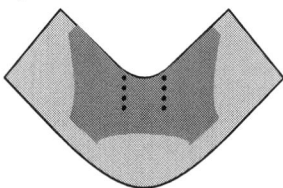

- With right sides together sew shoe to shoe lining all the way across the top of the shoe. Use a ⅛" (3 mm) seam. The webbing side of the lining should be on the outside and should not be touching the sneaker fabric.
- Clip curve at the three places indicated on the seam that you have just sewn.

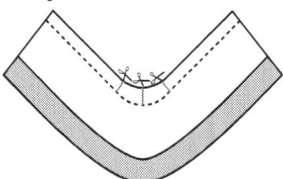

- Remove the backing from the fusible webbing.
- Turn the sneaker right side out so that the raw edges of the seam that you have just sewn are hidden. The webbing side of the lining should now be touching the wrong side of the sneaker fabric.
- Press to fuse the lining to the shoe.
- Use a narrow, close zigzag stitch and black thread to stitch around the outside of the overlay.

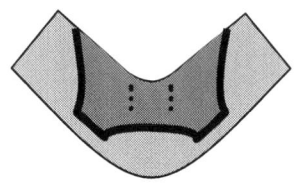

- Use a large needle to push through each of the eyelet holes printed on the sneaker.
- Thread the needle with pearl cotton and thread the cotton through the eyelets like a shoe lace.

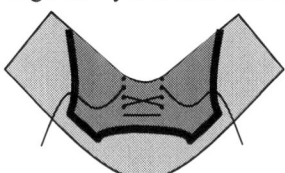

- Tie the cotton lace in a bow and trim the excess.
- Use white sewing thread to stitch through the center of the bow to prevent it from coming untied (optional).
- Right sides together, bring the two short sides of the sneaker together. Sew the ⅛" (3 mm) seam to make the sneaker heel.
- Turn the shoe right side out.

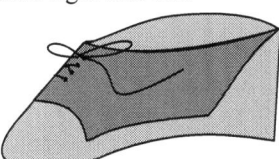

- Go to the section titled **Gluing the Sole and Insole**.

Boot

Cutting and Marking

- Cut out two boots and two boot linings.
- Cut out two soles from stiff felt.
- Cut out two insoles from an index card.

Sewing the Boot

- Back lining fabric with fusible webbing.
- Line up the boot lining below the facing for the boot top.
- Press to fuse the lining to the boot.

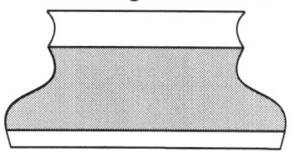

- With right sides together fold the top facing down. Match the A points to the B points.

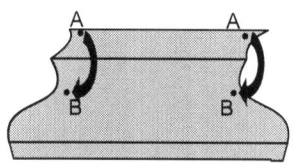

- Sew the curves.

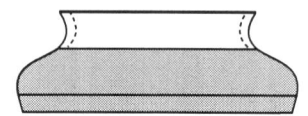

- Turn the facing to the inside of the boot.
- Fold the boot right sides together.
- Start at the end of the facing and sew the toe seam.

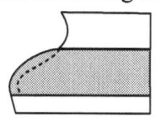

- Turn the boot right side out.
- Put seam sealant around the bottom of the boot and let dry. (optional)
- Go to the section titled **Gluing the Sole and Insole**.

Gluing the Sole and Insole

In this part of the instructions the word "vamp" refers to the top part of the shoe, slipper, sneaker, or boot.

- Clip the bottom of the vamp in the four places shown on the pattern. Stop each clip where the lining begins or at the slipper's stay stitching.

- Hand stitch and gather the heel and toe fabric at the bottom of the vamp until it curls around to the lining or the slipper's stay stitching. The stitching should be very close to the cut edge.

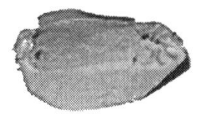

- Place the vamp on the shoe last or the doll's foot.
- Insert insole into the vamp.

- Glue the vamp bottom to the insole.
- Glue the sole to the outside of the vamp against the insole, hiding the insole and the vamp bottom.

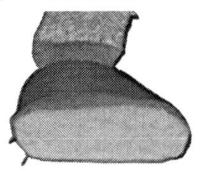

- You may zigzag narrow lace to the sock instead of hemming if you like. For a lettuce edge stretch the knit fabric as you attach the lace.

Sewing the Sock

- Refold each sock so that the right sides are together.
- Use a narrow zigzag stitch to sew from the top of the sock down the side and around the foot to the toe.

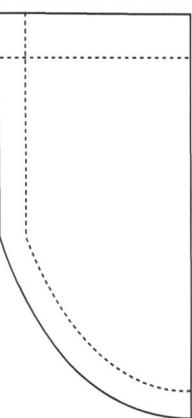

- Turn the sock right side out.

Sock

Cutting and Marking

- Cut socks on the fold.
- If you are using a sock for your source of knit fabric, you can place the top of the sock pattern at the finished top of your sock. Then you can skip the *Finishing the Top* section of the instructions and go straight to *Sewing the Sock*.

Finishing the Top

- To finish the top, open the folded fabric and turn ⅛" (3 mm) of fabric to the wrong side of the sock and zigzag.

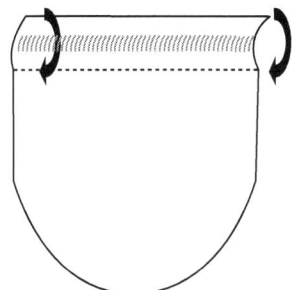

Shoes and Socks

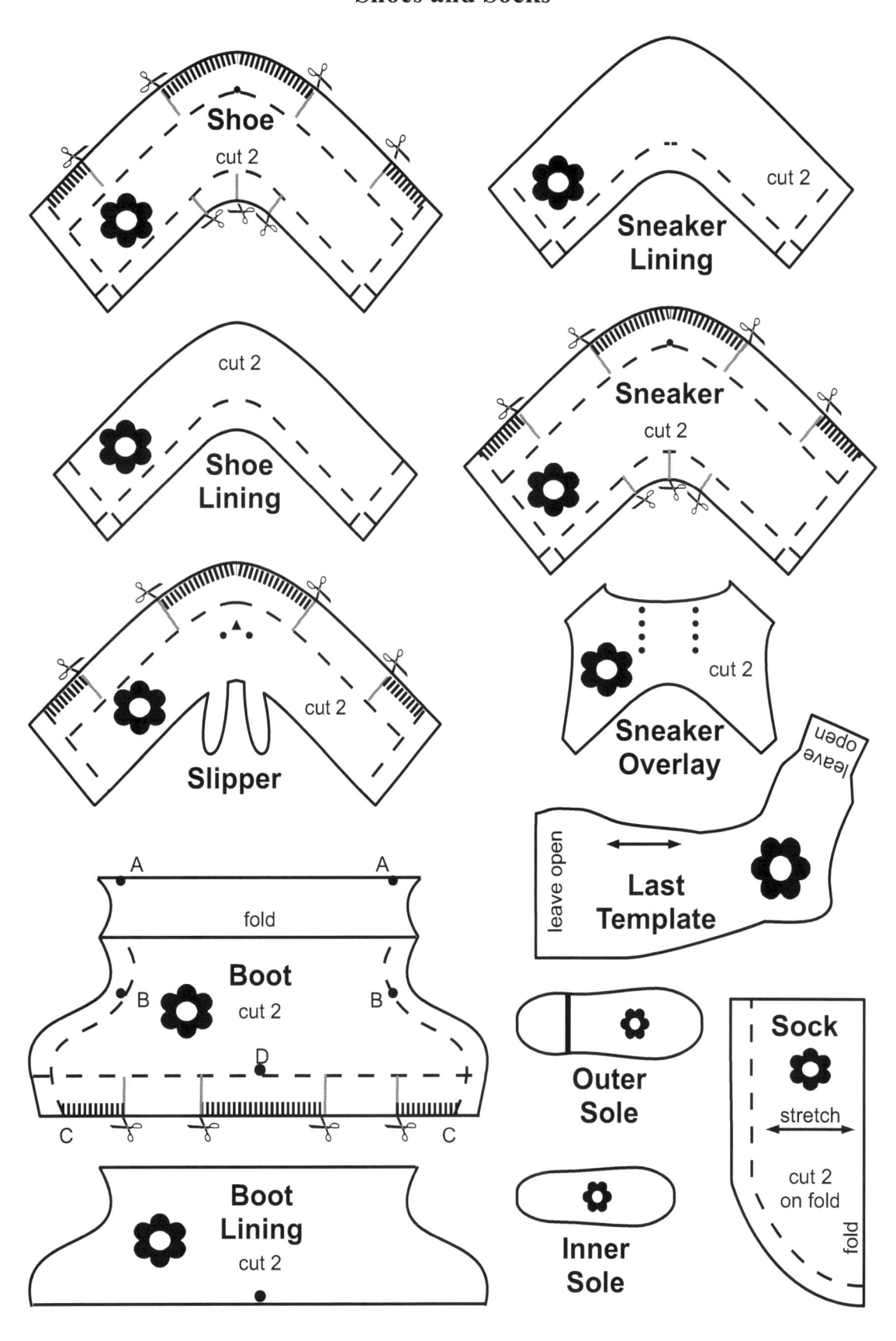

60

Sewing a Small Doll and Her Clothing
www.sherralynsdolls.com

Sewing Tools, Tips, and Techniques

APPENDIX

The following hints have been taken from my blog and revised for the sake of continuity. Occasionally a note in my patterns will refer you to topics in this section. The topic **Basic Sewing Tools**, for example, is listed under equipment in all my patterns.

I have written other hints hoping that they might be helpful to you as you sew Florabunda and her clothing. Some of the short cuts that I use are not traditional methods. If you prefer traditional methods, please use them.

Sewing Tools..62

Stitches..63

Marking Fabric..66

Finishing Raw Edges...67

Casings..68

Closures...69

Sewing Tools

Sewing Machine

- It is much easier to sew small doll clothes and cloth dolls if you use a sewing machine with controllable speed. A sewing machine that only has a fast speed is hard to maneuver while you are sewing short seams and small curves.
- A zigzag stitch is a must for sewing knits. Zigzagging is an easy way to finish seams on tiny doll clothes.

Basic Sewing Basket

I like sewing gadgets. I keep them in boxes and drawers all over my sewing room. If I were furnishing a sewing basket with basic sewing tools, I would list: dressmaker scissors, an assortment of pins and a pin cushion, an assortment of hand sewing needles, a thimble, and a tape measure.

- It is important that scissors are sharp and well made. I have both Gingher® and Fiskars® dressmaker shears. I can recommend either pair.

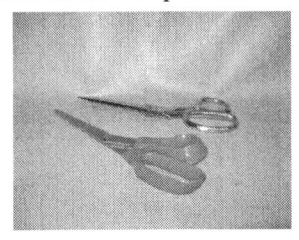

- I usually use glass head silk pins, but sometimes I use silk pins with a smaller metal head. I have an over sized tomato pin cushion and now a globe pin cushion made from the free pattern offered on my website.

- I have an assortment of hand sewing needles. Different sewing jobs need different size needles. The needle I use most often for hand sewing is a size 8 embroidery needle. For some jobs I may choose a longer or thinner needle. Occasionally I list an unusual size needle under equipment at the beginning of a pattern.
- Not everyone uses a thimble, but I can't get along without one.
- Along with my regular width tape measure I have a narrow tape measure made to use in dollmaking.

I have a few more tools that I use frequently. I have even more gadgets that I enjoy using at times. The tools that I have named are the ones that are used in most of my doll and doll clothes patterns.

Basic Ironing

It is as important to press seams between sewing steps in doll dressmaking as it is to press while making larger projects. Basic Ironing equipment is essential to sewing.
- Steam iron
- Full size ironing board
- Spray water bottle for moistening fabric if you are not using steam in your iron

More Sewing Tools

Here is a list of other sewing tools that are useful. Occasionally I list one of these tools under equipment at the beginning of a pattern.

Sewing Machine Tools

- Open embroidery foot

I use this foot when I am sewing a traced shape such as an arm or leg. The foot's openness makes the line easy to see.
- Ott-lite®

I have an Ott-lite on my sewing table. I use it along with my open embroidery foot to stitch a traced shape.
- Patchwork foot

This foot was made for quilters, but it is great for sewing ¼" (6 mm) and ⅛" (3 mm) seam allowances on doll clothes.
- Zipper foot

More Sewing basket

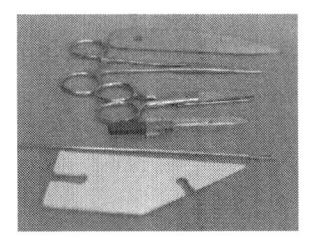

The picture shows a collection of tools that I find helpful.

- There are two different point turners in the picture.
   - The one at the top of the picture is helpful when turning curved pieces.
   - The bottom turner is helpful for defining sharp angles.
   - Both turners are helpful for defining points.

- The second tool from the top is a hemostat. It is helpful for turning small fabric pieces and stuffing dolls and toys.
- I use my small scissors for clipping seams and delicate trimming.
- A seam ripper is very useful to me. I need it more often than I like to admit.
- The bodkin makes it easy to insert elastic into a casing.

More Ironing

- Doll Clothes Ironing Board

I have a small ironing board made for pressing doll clothes that I find very useful. It makes pressing little sleeves and hems easier.

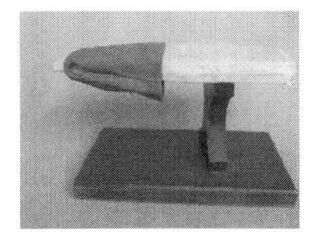

- A Sleeve Roll

A sleeve roll is sometimes a good choice for pressing small sewing projects, because small pieces may be pinned to it. I push the pins straight down into the roll as if it were a pin cushion.

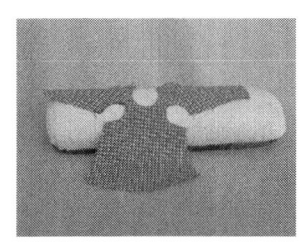

- Pressing strips

Cut ½" (12 mm) wide strips from a 5" x 8" (or metric equivalent) index card printed with a ¼" (6 mm) grid. To accurately press under a ½" (12 mm) of fabric pull the edge of fabric over the paper strip and press. To press under ¼" (6 mm) of fabric pull the fabric to the ¼" (6 mm) line and press.

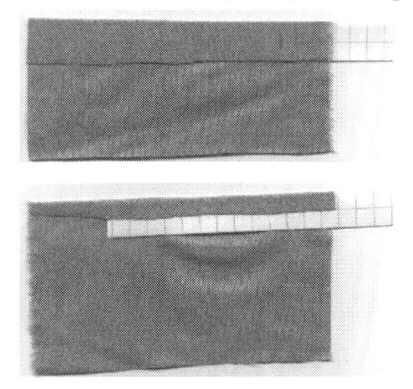

- Finger pressing

Sometimes in dollmaking the only pressing equipment that you need is a finger or two.
  - To finger press a seam open spread the seam open and run your index finger or thumb down the stitch line. Put enough pressure on the stitch to encourage the seam to stay open.
  - To finger press a crease in the fabric pinch the fabric between your finger and thumb at the spot where you want the crease to begin. Pull the fabric through your finger and thumb along the line to be creased. If you are not satisfied with the crease, repeat the pinch and pull process.

Stitches

Machine Stitches

- Stay stitching
  - Stay stitching is usually sewn on the stitching line of a single layer of fabric.
  - It is used to prevent fabric from stretching.
  - It is used as a guide for folding or clipping fabric.

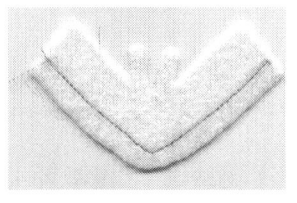

- Topstitching
  - Topstitching will be visible on a finished garment.
  - Use the edge of the presser foot or a seam guide to produce a straight stitch.
  - Match the thread color to the fabric or choose an interesting contrast.

- Gathering stitch
  - Sew two parallel rows of long stitches and pull the bobbin threads until the fabric is gathered to the desired length.
  - Check the fabric to see if the stitches can be removed from the fabric without leaving small holes. Then one row of gathering stitches may use a ⅜" (9 mm) seam guide even though the joining seam will be ¼" (6 mm). Remove the visible gathering stitch after the joining seam has been sewn.
- Zigzag stitch
  - Joining knits fabric
    - Use zigzag stitches to join knit fabric. I have not had success using a serger to join very small knit pieces.
    - Use a fairly wide zigzag stitch to join knits. Set the zigzags to be fairly close together, but not a satin stitch.

- If your zigzag is not as wide as the seam allowance, you may trim the seam. 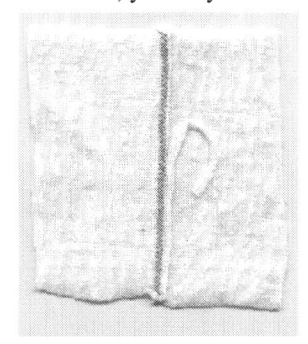
- Sewing lace to knits with the zigzag stitch
  - Lay the lace on the right side of the fabric.
  - If the lace will extend above or below the fabric, overlap the raw edge of the knit with the lace heading. 
  - If the lace will lie on top of the fabric make the heading even with the raw edge.
  - Stitch a narrow almost satin stitch on the lace heading.

Hand Stitching

One stitch is defined as the needle going into and coming out of the fabric.
- Running stitch

Several stitches are made with the needle before the thread is pulled through the fabric.

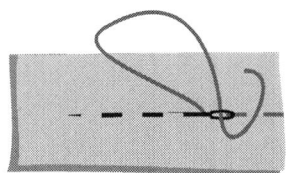

- Basting stitches

Basting stitches are running stitches used to hold fabric together so that it can be sewn with a machine stitch.
- Hand Gathering

Hand gathering stitches are running stitches that are pulled so that the fabric is gathered over the thread.
- Slip-Stitch
  - A slip-stitch is an almost invisible stitch. It is a good stitch to use when putting in a hem.
  - Finish the raw edge of the garment to be hemmed.
  - Press in the hem. For these small doll patterns the hem is usually ½" (12 mm).
  - Use a few pins to hold the hem in place.
  - Check the length on the doll before continuing.
  - Fold the finished edge back about ⅛" (3 mm). 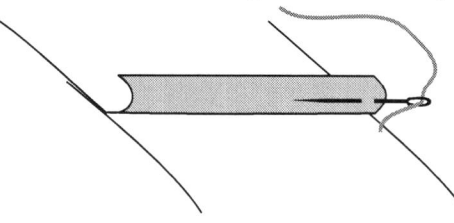
  - Take about an ⅛" (3 mm) stitch through the folded back edge. Pull the thread through the fabric.
  - Catch two or three threads and take a small stitch on the part of the hem that will be visible on the dress.
  - Take the next stitch in the folded back edge. For these small hems the visible stitches should about ¼" (6 mm) apart.

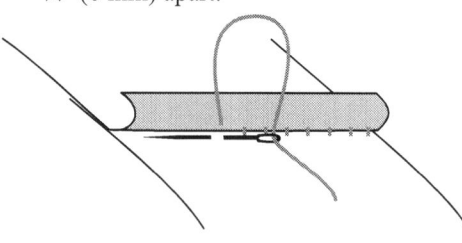

- Ladder Stitch

In doll patterns and doll crafting magazines the invisible hand stitch used in doll construction is called the ladder stitch. In embroidery books the ladder stitch is a decorative stitch that looks like a ladder. The dollmaker's ladder stitch is similar to the slip-stitch, but it is done on the outside of the doll.
- Using the ladder stitch to connect the doll's head to the body
  - Insert the neck into the opening in the head.
  - Use a few pins if you like to hold the two parts together. I usually just hold the two together as I sew.
  - Take a small stitch in the head.
  - Pull the thread through each stitch as you take it.
  - Take the second stitch in the neck.
  - Go back to the head for the next stitch and make it very close to the first stitch.
  - Continue back and forth.
  - Take only one stitch at a time. Pull the thread completely through with each stitch.

- Keep the stitches very close together. You should take between fifteen and twenty stitches per inch.

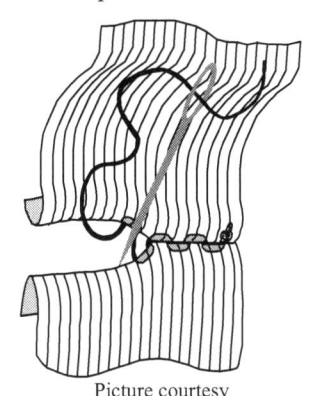

Picture courtesy
Dover Publications
"Easy to Make Story Book Dolls"
by Sherralyn St. Clair

- Sewing arm and leg stuffing openings closed with the ladder stitch
    - Finish stuffing each piece.
    - Tuck the raw edges of the stuffing opening inside the arm or leg.
    - Hold the edges of the stuffing opening together as you sew.
    - Do not overlap the edges as you sew.
    - Take a small stitch on one side of the opening.
    - Pull the thread through each stitch as you take it.
    - Take the second stitch on the other side of the opening.
    - Go back to first side for the next stitch and make it very close to the beginning stitch.
    - Continue back and forth. Keep the stitches very close together. You should take between fifteen and twenty stitches per inch.
- Overcasting Stitch
    - Using overcasting to close a body back stuffing opening
        - Start sewing at the top of the stuffing opening on the left side of the opening. Hide the thread knot by inserting the needle into the top of the stuffing opening and bringing it out on the left side.
        - Make a stitch straight across the opening to the right side.
        - Make the second stitch going right to left slightly slanted. The second stitch in each pair will be inside the closing, so that the visible stitches go straight across the stuffing opening.
        - Continue back and forth keeping the outside stitching straight

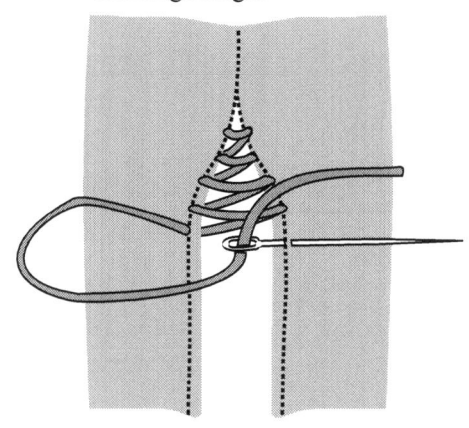

    - Pull the stitches tight as you sew. The above figure shows loose stitches to illustrate thread placement.
    - Using overcasting to close an arm or leg
        - Finish stuffing each piece.
        - Tuck the raw edges of the stuffing opening inside the arm or leg.
        - Hold the edges of the stuffing opening together as you sew.
        - Sew both sides of the opening together with each stitch.
        - Keep the stitches small and close together.

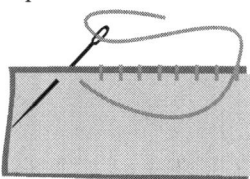

- French Knot

The French knot is the embroidery stitch used for the bunny's eyes in the bunny slippers. The books I have read have different opinions on the number of times to wrap the floss around the needle while making the stitch. One book says only one wrap. One book says one or two. Another book says two or three wraps. I decided to use the average of two wraps for the bunny's eyes. To make thicker French knots, use more strands of floss.
    - Bring the needle to the right side of the fabric slightly to the right of the point marked for the French knot.
    - Pull all the floss through the fabric until it stops at the knotted end.
    - Hold the needle close to the marked point and wrap the floss around the needle twice.

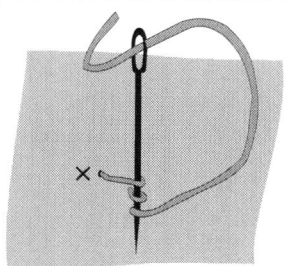

- Insert the needle through the point marked on the fabric.

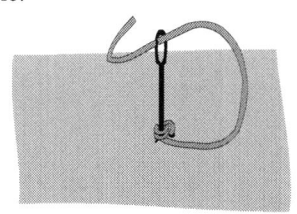

Marking Fabric

First choose a pen, pencil, or other method to mark your fabric pieces. Then choose the method to use for transferring the pattern markings to the fabric. You can find other more traditional methods for marking fabric in sewing handbooks.

Choosing pens and pencils

- Use a thin line air soluble pen when marking on the right side of the fabric. I find that the thicker air soluble pens are not precise enough for marking small size sewing projects. Mark with this type of pen just before sewing, because it disappears quickly. Sometimes the markings will last a few hours or a few days zipped in an air tight plastic bag. The time the marking lasts depends on the age of the pen and the amount of humidity in the air.
- For marks on the wrong side of the fabric and marks for embroidery designs, I like to use Prismacolor® pencils. They wash out easily.
- If you prefer more traditional marking methods, you can purchase tailor's chalk in various colors, or try a marking wheel and transfer paper.

Tracing Markings

- Hold the pattern and fabric up to a window to trace markings. This method is easier if the pattern and fabric are held to the window with drafting tape. (I think masking tape is too strong.)
- A clear plastic box picture frame works fairly well when tracing pattern markings. It should be propped up at an angle rather than resting flat on a table. Another solution is to have a battery powered light under the plastic box. Light should be behind the pattern that you are tracing.
- My favorite tracing method is a light box or table. I bought a small inexpensive one years ago. Larger ones may be fairly pricey. I use a small amount of drafting tape to hold the pattern and fabric to my light box.

Clipping fabric

- Cut out the small notches in the seam allowance that are used to help match fabric pieces. 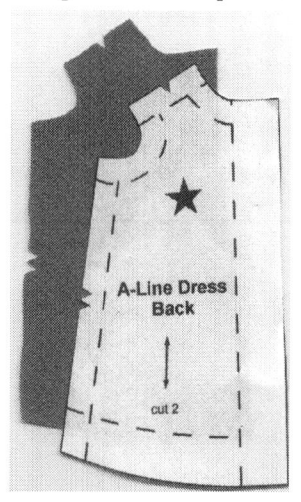
- You can make a small clip in the middle of each notch if you prefer.

Cutting out Parts of a Paper Pattern

- Darts
    - Rather than tracing darts you can print out or copy a second pattern piece.
    - Cut the dart shape out of the pattern.
    - Place the pattern on the fabric piece to be marked.
    - Trace the dart where it belongs on the pattern. 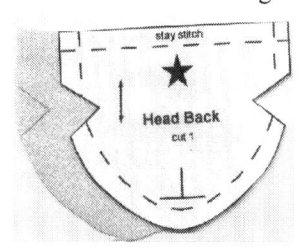
- Dots
    - Pull a pin with a small metal head through the dot on the paper pattern.
    - Put the pattern on the fabric to be marked.
    - Use a pen or pencil to mark the fabric through the hole in the pattern.

Finishing Raw Edges

Serger

- Finishing two raw edges together
    - Sew the seam with a straight stitch on a sewing machine.
    - Serge using only three spools of thread. This method produces a narrow finished seam and a small stitch connecting the fabric pieces. Serge close to the machine stitching so that the serger knife will trim the seam to about ⅛" (3 mm). Note that the bottom of the sample has not been serged to show how the serger knife has narrowed the seam. 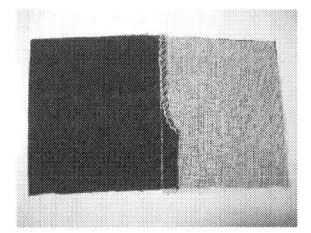
    - Add a drop of seam sealant on the stitching at the beginning and end of each line of serging.
    - Press the seam to one side.
    - Small curves such as those on sleeves and necklines of doll clothing are difficult to do with a serger.
- Finishing single edges in hems and casings
    - Use only three thread spools to make a narrow finish.
    - Sew near the edge so that the fabric is not cut with the knife.
    - Turn up the hem the desired amount and slip-stitch. 
    - For hems in A-line garments add a machine gathering stitch next to the finished edge.
    - Pull the gathering thread until the hem lies flat against the skirt and slip-stitch.

Zigzag Stitch

- Finishing two raw edges together
    - Sew the seam with a straight stitch. 
    - Set the zigzag stitch about ⅛" (3 mm) wide.
    - Make the zigzags close together, but not a satin stitch.
    - Zigzag close to the straight stitch so that there is about an ⅛" (3 mm) raw edge.
    - Trim the seam close to the finished edge. 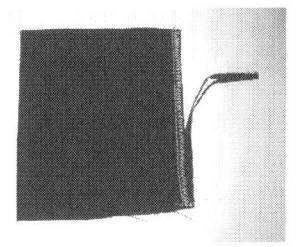
    - Press the seam to one side. 
- Finishing single edges in hems and casings
    - Sew near the edge to be finished.

- Turn up the hem the desired amount and slip-stitch.

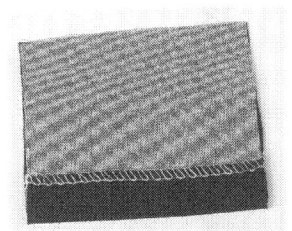

- For hems in A line garments add a machine gathering stitch next to the finished edge
- Pull the gathering thread until the hem lies flat against the skirt and slip-stitch.

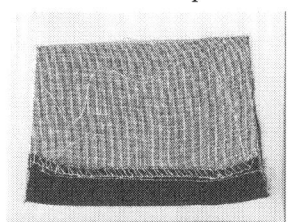

Pinking Shears

- Small curves such as those on sleeves and necklines of doll clothing are difficult to cut with pinking shears.
- Pink the seam close to the raw edge. The measurement from the peak of the pinked edge to the stitch should be almost ¼" (6 mm).
- These seams may be pressed open unless they are inside an elastic casing.

- The Pinked edges may be pressed in the same direction so that the machine stitching is visible inside the garment. The edges must be pressed in one direction if they will be inside an elastic casing.

Using a seam sealant to finish seams

- Lay the cut pieces that you want to treat on a sheet of wax paper.
- Squeeze a few drops of seam sealant onto the wax paper. I have tried applying the sealant directly to the fabric, but I always ended up with too much on the edges. Too much sealant makes the fabric edges stiff and difficult to sew through.
- Use a toothpick to apply a small amount to the outside edges of the fabric pieces.
- To make the sealed edges softer, after the sealant has dried, soak the treated pieces in a bowl of water. After five or ten minutes remove the fabric from the water. Blot the pieces and let air dry. Press. The fabric is soft and easy to sew. This soaking step is optional.
- These seams may be pressed open unless they are inside an elastic casing.

Casings

- To insert elastic into doll clothes casings I always use ⅛" (3 mm) elastic and my favorite bodkin.

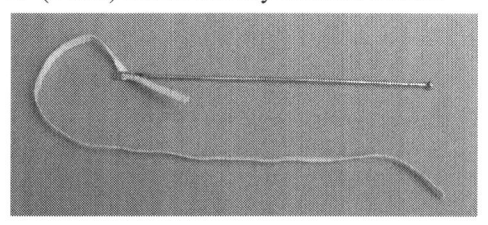

- Use your whole length of elastic. Do not cut it until it is secure on both sides of the casing. Use a bodkin to pull the elastic through the casing.
- If a seam is inside the casing, the two seam edges should have been finished together and pressed to one side. The bodkin should travel over the stitching first and then over the two seams.

- Pull the elastic through the casing with the bodkin.
- Release the elastic from the bodkin and secure the released end to the casing by sewing through it several times.

- Check the pattern instructions for measurement. Gather the casing fabric over the elastic to the desired length without stretching the elastic.
- Try the garment on to check the size.

- Secure the second side of the elastic to the second casing opening by sewing through it and the casing several times.

- Cut off the excess elastic.

Closures

Closing the Back With Hook and Loop Tape

I like to close garments for small dolls with short pieces of hook and loop tape. In this method the left and right sides of the closing will be side by side like a zipper closing rather than overlapping like closings with buttons or snaps. I do not use the overlap method for hook and loop tape in these patterns, because the overlapped closing is too thick on such small dresses.

- Use your favorite method to finish each side of the opening.
- Press each finished side of the opening ½" (12 mm) to the inside.
- Take a 1" (2.5 cm) length of ¾" (18 mm) wide hook and loop tape. The hook side and the loop side of the tape should be fastened.
- Split this tape in half lengthwise so that there are two 1" (2.5 cm) lengths of ⅜" (9 mm) tape.

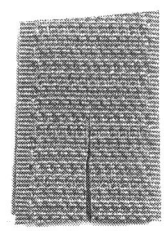

- Separate the tape into the hook and loop sides.

- Take the hook side of one of the tape pairs and lay it face up partly under the right side of the opening at the top of the opening. About ¼" (6 mm) of tape should stick out of the opening and about ⅛" (3 mm) of the tape should be under the fabric edge of the opening. The bumpy hook side of the tape should be touching the fabric at this ⅛" (3 mm) overlap.

- At the edge of the right back opening stitch through the fabric and the tape.
- Lay the first piece of loop tape completely inside the left side of the back opening. The loops should be out and the smooth side of the tape should be against the fabric.
- Stitch down the tape through the fabric.
- At ⅛" (3 mm) from the bottom of the tape, pivot on the needle and stitch a few horizontal stitches.
- Pivot on the needle again and stitch back up the tape.

- For garments that need a second strip of hook and loop tape measure ½" (12 mm) down from the first piece of loop tape and sew the second piece of tape in the same manner as the first tape.

- I like to use snag free Velcro®. The snag free variety sticks to itself, so you don't need to worry about hook and loop sides. To use this type of tape, split a single 1" (2.5 cm) length of tape in half lengthwise so that you have two narrow 1" (2.5 cm) lengths. Use one piece in place of the hook side and one piece in place of the loop side in the above instructions.

Closing the Back with Snaps

If you prefer an overlapped closing, use small snaps.
- Press under ½" (12 mm) at back left closing and ¼" (6 mm) at back right closing.
- Overlap right over left ¼" (6 mm).
- Check fit on doll before applying snaps.
- Use two to four snaps to close dress.

Other Books by Sherralyn St. Clair

Sewing for Large Dolls - Full size Patterns for 18" Doll Outfits

This book is a collection of patterns for large 18" (46 cm) dolls. The book includes full size patterns and detailed sewing instructions for the Kitty cloth doll and her outfits. In addition to Sherralyn's Dolls Kitty, the outfits will fit American Girl® dolls, Springfield® Collection dolls, and other 18" dolls. Measurements are given in both US and metric units.

The patterns include: Nightgown and Sleep Cap; A-line Dress, and Jacket; Pants, Shorts, Skirt, and T-shirt; Ballgown and Classic Dress; Shoes, Slippers, Sandals, Sneakers, and Six Styles of Bedroom Slippers; as well as Kitty Cloth Doll, Camisole, and Panties. Most of these patterns match those found in *Sewing for Mini Dolls*.

Sherralyn's Tools, Tips, and Techniques is included.

Sewing for Mini Dolls - Full size patterns for 6½" mini doll outfits

This book is a collection of patterns for mini dolls (6½" or 16.5 cm). The book includes full size patterns and detailed sewing instructions for the Twinkle cloth doll and her outfits. In addition to Sherralyn's Dolls Twinkle, the outfits will fit American Girl® Mini and other mini dolls. Measurements are given in both US and metric units.

The patterns include: Nightgown, Smock Top, and Two Tiered Skirt; A-line Dress, Jacket, and Bloomers; Pants, Shorts, Skirt, and T-shirt; Ballgown and Classic Dress; Shoes, Slippers, Sandals, Sneakers, and Boots; as well as Twinkle Cloth Mini Doll, Camisole, and Panties. Most of these patterns match those found in *Sewing for Large Dolls*

Sherralyn's Tools, Tips, and Techniques is included.

Learn to Sew for Your Doll - A Beginner's Guide to Sewing for an 18" Doll

If you would like to teach a special child how to sew, this book presents a series of skills in a learning sequence that takes the new seamstress from the first use of a sewing machine through making an attractive wardrobe for a doll. The book gives the student a place to start and then builds on the initial skills.

This book includes instructions and full size patterns for 18" doll clothes. Measurements are given in both US and metric units.

Skills taught include: pattern reading and cutting, machine stitching, finishing seams, gathering, sewing casings, topstitching, hemming, and attaching closures.

Easy-to-Make Storybook Dolls - A "Novel" Approach to Cloth Dollmaking

This unique guide to making 14" cloth dolls offers patterns for the eternal optimist, Pollyanna, as well as Dorothy from *The Wonderful Wizard of Oz* and Mary of *The Secret Garden*. Perfect for beginners, this manual will also appeal to more experienced dollmakers.

All three characters use the same basic doll body and accessories such as hats, shoes, and slips. Dorothy's wardrobe, based on descriptions of her clothing in Oz books, comprises six dresses and a nightgown. Mary's ensemble includes five dresses, a coat, and a housecoat; and Pollyanna's costumes consist of six dresses and a gown. Extras include Dorothy's green spectacles and Toto the terrier; a bed cover, and a pillow for Mary; and Pollyanna's pets, Fluffy the cat and Buffy the dog.

Sherralyn's Dolls

Visit my web site at www.sherralynsdolls.com to get more fun out of your pattern books. Here's some of what you can find there.

Patterns

The Patterns page contains patterns for doll clothes, accessories, and cloth dolls of various sizes. Many of the patterns in my books can be purchased separately for download from this web page.

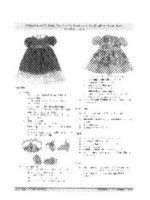

You can also find a free sundress pattern for three sizes of small dolls, a free sewing tips booklet, and free miniature quilt block patterns.

Florabunda's Page

This page is kid friendly with a music video and fun surprises.

It has free sewing and craft projects that let kids make accessories for themselves and their dolls.

My free stories can inspire kids to use their dolls for creative play.

My Books

On My Books page you can find color versions of outfits from the books. E-mail me whenever you have sewing questions.

Blog

Check my blog page for sewing hints and thoughts on sewing. Feel free to leave a comment and start a discussion.

Printed in Great Britain
by Amazon.co.uk, Ltd.,
Marston Gate.